Priester's Presents

Dining on the

Victorian
VERANDAH

A Cup of Good Wishes
Jane Westbrook

To Order Additional Books:

Dining on the Victorian Verandah

PRIESTER'S PECAN COMPANY, INC.
P. O. Drawer 381
Fort Deposit, Alabama 36032
Toll Free 1-800-277-3226

Additional Cookbooks by Gene Westbrook:

THE MAGNOLIA COLLECTION
PIGSKIN PARTIES
POSITIVELY PEACHY

SEPTEMBER 1996   **FIRST EDITION**   10,000 COPIES

———— by ————
GENE WESTBROOK

Book Cover Design and Illustrations by GENIA WESTBROOK CLEMENTS

Page Illustrations by GARY W. CLEMENTS

Cover Watercolor by DEBBIE WITT

Edited by ISABELLE V. HANSON

Printed in the U. S. A.

Library of Congress Catalog Card Number 96-90457
ISBN 0-9614247-3-7

About the Author

A native Alabamian, Gene Westbrook attended Mary Washington College of the University of Virginia and the University of Alabama. Gene has achieved acclaim for her entertaining and marvelous collection of recipes. Her cookbooks evolved from her many interests and associations with a wide variety of people. You never know where she might be creating her next recipes -- be it by the campfire, while backpacking across the Continental Divide, or at her next book signing. She has a magnetic, Italian-mother personality, which extends far beyond her nuclear family. She is forever inviting new people home for Christmas dinner served with true Southern hospitality.

The author's entire family helps bring her cookbooks into being. Her daughter, Genia, designs the books; her husband, Joe, is the photographer and publisher; and her two sons, Almand and Jay, have the enviable job of chief tasters. And, of course, Gene's mother and father taught her how to plan a fun and food-filled party. Needless to say, Oxford and Major, the author's dogs, have enjoyed many years of delectable table scraps!

Gene and Joe reside in the small community of Robinson Springs, outside the capital city of Montgomery, Alabama.

About the Book
Designer & Illustrator

Genia Westbrook Clements is my daughter first and foremost. I have the good fortune of being the mother of a very talented artist, illustrator, and visual designer.

A graduate of Auburn University with a Bachelor of Fine Arts degree, she and her illustrator husband, Gary, own a visual arts studio. Their home and business studio are located on a high hill overlooking their horse farm near Prattville, Alabama.

Genia is also an avid kayaker and certified American Canoe & Kayak Association instructor. Look for the blonde in a kayak on the river catching an eddy after having successfully run a rapid named "Screaming Left Turn!"

Her artistic talents add the beautiful visual "topping" to our cookbook.

Foreword

I always find it interesting to know the origins of a book. What sparked the initial interest to begin? The American Dream and entrepreneurial spirit is often derived from small towns and within close families. This has definitely been the derivation of this cookbook, which blends the recipes of the L. C. Priester Family, the H. R. Ellis Family, and my family, the A. J. Westbrooks.

The Westbrook home is near the tiny community of Robinson Springs, about 12 miles north of Montgomery, Alabama, where I write and publish cookbooks.

One of my very earliest wholesale customers for my first cookbook was Priester's Pecan Company's retail store. Through the years of this association, I became friends with one of the owners and the manager of the retail operations, Ellen Ellis Burkett.

Ellen had long wanted a cookbook for their company, with some of the Ellis Family recipes. In 1995, Ellen and I began planning the presentation of this cookbook for your enjoyment.

Our cookbook combines recipes from the Ellis Family, their friends, and their employees, along with recipes from my family, friends, and some originals of my own.

All of the recipes in this cookbook have been tested for accuracy, ease, and success in making. We all sincerely hope that you will find excellence and enjoyment throughout our cookbook.

It comes to you with a cup of good wishes, Jene

Table of Contents

The Road Ran Through It

Let me tell you a little about a handshake partnership and Priester's Pecan Company. Alabama's largest handmade gourmet candy company began about 1935 in Fort Deposit, Alabama. This small town of approximately 1,200 people was founded as a Revolutionary War ammunition depository. It is located just off of I-65, about 35 miles south of Montgomery, Alabama.

Mr. Lee C. Priester owned and operated a Texaco service station on the main highway between Mobile and Montgomery, Alabama. He had a traveling trade that often stopped for more than gasoline. His customers wanted refreshments and a touch of the South to take along with them.

Fort Deposit had a generous supply of pecan trees in the area, and Mr. Priester realized that pecans might be a good addition to his business, since pecans were a much-sought-after delicacy. Mr. Priester, or L. C. as he was always called, hired a local man, Caesar, to knock the ripened pecans down from the trees with a long stick. Caesar would bring his sacks of pecans to the porch of L. C.'s home, located next door to the service station. The pecans in the shells were bagged there on the porch for sale next door at the service station. No one is sure exactly when "Special Order Number One" was placed, but a salesman stopped to buy gasoline one day and asked L. C. for a special favor. He wanted the pecans cracked and shelled to be picked up upon his return from his business trip. L. C., being a good businessman, said it would be done. He proceeded to contract some of the local ladies to crack and shell some of the pecans. Thus began the real Priester's Pecan Company from that customer's request! The pecan business grew with Mrs. Priester's assistance, along with the local ladies, until the back porch could no longer handle the volume. A larger facility was bought.

As business continued to grow, L. C. realized the need for a financial partner. He selected his longtime friend and business associate Hence Reynolds Ellis.

Hence owned the oil distributorship that supplied L.C.'s service station and a saw mill. He had served as both mayor of Fort Deposit and as a board member at the local bank.

With a simple handshake, and an initial loan of $200, Hence became the silent partner in Priester's Pecan Company.

Hence and his wife, Ellen Hagood Ellis, eventually brought their two sons, Ned and John, along with their wives, May and Rose, into the business. Hence continued his involvement in the business until his death in 1965; likewise, L. C. remained in the business until illness forced his retirement.

The addition of the sheer manpower of the Ellis Clan, especially during the Christmas rush season, was a major springboard for the success of the early company.

John Ellis went on to other pursuits as a banker and businessman, while his brother, Ned, took over the management of Priester's Pecan Company. Ned eventually bought the entire business.

Ned Ellis, like his father, has been successfully involved in quite a number of businesses. An Auburn University graduate and distinguished military veteran, Ned has been a bank organizer, civic and religious leader, cattle rancher, dairy farmer, and poultry producer on his 3,000-acre Circle E Farms. He has also served as a board member and office holder for various national beef and pecan organizations.

Throughout the years, Ned's wife, May, has provided all manner of assistance in the growth of the pecan company, plus being a schoolteacher, wife, and mother. She is currently co-owner, with their daughter Ellen, of The Pineapple Gift Shops in two cities.

Ned and May's four children -- Marsha, Katie, Thomas, and Ellen -- have all played a part in this American Dream of building a high-quality product business.

Today's Priester's Pecan Company is managed by Thomas Ellis and Ellen Ellis Burkett. They both began "helping" at the company at about age 10. And now it seems that Tyler, Stinson, and Taber Ellis, and Salley and Cliff Burkett will continue the American Dream family-business tradition of the very finest quality products.

Appetizers

Crab Ravigotte

1/2 cup mayonnaise	1 tablespoon chopped pimento
1 tablespoon finely minced parsley	1 hard-boiled egg, finely chopped
1 tablespoon drained capers, chopped	1 teaspoon lemon juice
1-1/2 teaspoons dry mustard	1 lb. fresh crabmeat (lump is best)
1-1/2 teaspoons prepared horseradish	Salt to taste
	Garnish: sweet red and green pepper strips

In a large bowl, mix all ingredients except crabmeat and garnish until well blended. Add the crabmeat, and lightly toss to blend. Salt to taste. Garnish top with criss-crossed sweet red and green pepper strips. Serve on Crispy Triangles (see recipe page 12) or crackers.

Peppered Tenderloin

Marinate overnight.

4 tablespoons coarsely ground
  black pepper
4 lbs. beef tenderloin (may be one
  or more pieces)
2/3 cup soy sauce

1/2 cup vinegar
1 tablespoon tomato sauce
1 teaspoon paprika
1 medium clove garlic, minced

Spread the black pepper on the beef, and press into the meat, coating the entire surface. Place the beef in a glass baking dish just large enough to hold the beef and marinade. Combine soy sauce, vinegar, tomato sauce, paprika, and garlic; mix well. Carefully spoon the sauce over the peppered beef to avoid loosening the pepper. Cover and refrigerate overnight; turn once. When ready to cook, remove beef from the sauce, and grill or broil to desired doneness. Slice beef thin to serve. Serve on thinly sliced fresh French baguette rounds with horseradish mayonnaise.

Horseradish Mayonnaise

Pure ground horseradish
  (not creamed)
Mayonnaise

Put the horseradish into a small crystal or glass bowl; then stir in the mayonnaise to taste. Keep in mind that the horseradish gains in horsepower as it begins to blend!

Helen's Chili Hot Shrimp

Make 1 or 2 days in advance.

4 (8-oz.) packages cream cheese
1 lb. cooked shrimp, chopped
1 large onion, finely diced

3 cloves garlic, minced
2 medium peeled tomatoes, diced
1/2 fresh jalapeno pepper, diced

In a large skillet, over low heat, melt the cream cheese; then stir in all of the other ingredients. Simmer for 20 minutes. Allow mixture to cool; then refrigerate overnight. The next day test for jalapeno "hotness"; if it is not nippy enough add a bit more diced jalapeno. At serving time heat slowly on low heat. Serve warm with crispy triangles. Serves 25. *(see Crispy Triangles, Page 12.)*

Helen Carden, my sister by marriage, has collected some rather wonderful recipes from her military friends all over the world. She has been known to call from Europe or Washington at odd hours for a new recipe; that keeps life spicy like the chili pepper in her recipe. Her husband, Grif, really gave us a jolt when his only request for a stateside gift was for SPARE RIBS to be brought to Belgium. It seems the butchers there did not know how to cut them. Unfortunately for him, we "wimped-out," fearing those fierce Belgium customs officers. As it turns out, customs looked the other way when we arrived. Sorry, Grif, we could have brought a whole suitcase full!

chilled Bleu Grapes

Make early in the day to allow chilling time.

1/2 lb. seedless green grapes, washed and patted dry
8 oz. cream cheese, softened
4 oz. bleu cheese, crumbled
1/2 cup pecans, very finely chopped

Combine cream cheese and bleu cheese; blend completely. Form a small ball of the cheese mixture, flatten between palms of hands, and form around each grape. Roll grapes in the chopped pecans to coat, and place in a flat casserole dish. When all the grapes are made, cover dish and refrigerate until serving time.

Now this is a strange sounding recipe, but it is quite delicious. If you like the flavor of bleu cheese, it will definitely be a "go" for you.

Elizabeth's Crab Torte Appetizer

8 oz. cream cheese, softened
1 cup catsup
4 tablespoons horseradish
3 tablespoons lemon juice
2 drops Tabasco sauce
1 lb. fresh lump or claw crabmeat
1 fresh lemon

Select a pretty serving platter, and spread the cream cheese over the bottom in a layer. In a bowl, mix catsup, horseradish, lemon juice, and Tabasco sauce until well blended. Spread the catsup mixture over the cream cheese layer. Top with a layer of crabmeat. Squeeze the juice from the fresh lemon over the crabmeat. Cover and refrigerate until serving time. Serve cold with crackers.

Scalloped Mushrooms

24 oz. small whole mushrooms	2/3 of a (3-oz.) jar Hormel real
1 cup Italian bread crumbs	bacon bits (no imitation)
8 oz. grated Cheddar cheese,	1/2 cup mayonnaise
plus extra for garnish	1 (10-3/4-oz.) can cream of
8 green onions, thinly sliced	chicken or mushroom soup
with tops	2 tablespoons cooking sherry
	(optional)

Wash mushrooms, and trim the very bottoms of stems; pat mushrooms dry. Select a 9-x 13-inch baking dish that can be used as a serving dish; prepare with spray-oil. Sprinkle the bottom of the baking dish with a thin layer of 1/2 of the bread crumbs. In a bowl, mix the whole mushrooms with all the remaining ingredients. Spoon the mushroom mixture over the crumbs as evenly as possible. Top with additional grated Cheddar cheese. Bake at 350 degrees for 35 to 40 minutes. Serve hot in the baking dish with toothpicks on the side for skewering.

This recipe can also be served as a vegetable side dish for dinner. You may want to sprinkle the top with paprika and/or parsley flakes for color.

Crispy Triangles

Make well in advance; they can be stored for weeks.	1 loaf very thin white bread

Cut crusts from the loaf with an electric knife; then cut the loaf in half diagonally. Make one more diagonal cut in the opposite direction to make smaller triangles (4 triangles per slice of bread). Place triangles on cookie sheets, and bake at 250 degrees until light brown. Store in airtight container.

Auburn Stars

1 package wonton wrappers	1 (4-oz.) can chopped black
1 lb. light bulk sausage, hot or	olives
mild	1 cup finely grated Cheddar
1 cup prepared ranch salad	cheese
dressing	1 cup finely grated Monterey
1/2 sweet red pepper, diced	Jack cheese
1/2 green pepper, diced	

Preheat oven to 350 degrees. Spray the BOTTOM of mini-muffin tins with spray-oil (full-size muffin tins may also be used.) Fit the wonton wrappers over the bottoms of the muffin cups to resemble the shape of a 4-or 5-pointed star. Bake the stars on a mid-level oven rack for 5 minutes or until stars are stiff; set aside to cool. Cook the sausage until done; crumble and drain. Mix the remaining ingredients into the drained sausage. Remove the cooled stars to a spray-oil prepared baking pan. Fill the stars with the sausage mixture (fill larger stars about 2/3 full). While watching carefully, bake stars on lower oven rack in the preheated oven until mixture is bubbly, about 10 minutes. Makes 45 to 50.

This delicious and cleverly presented recipe was created by Mandy Pope Smith and promptly stolen by her sister, Liza Pope Peterson. What a pair these two Auburn University graduates are! Some think stars fell on Alabama, but these stars fell on Auburn!

Hot Spinach & Artichoke Dip

1 (10-oz.) package frozen chopped spinach	Salt to taste
2 tablespoons margarine	1 (14-oz.) can artichoke hearts, drained and chopped
1 small onion, finely chopped	8 oz. cream cheese, softened
1/2 teaspoon garlic powder	4 oz. Monterey Jack cheese, grated
1/4 teaspoon Worcestershire sauce	1 cup grated Parmesan cheese
1/4 teaspoon Tabasco sauce	1 cup mayonnaise

Place the frozen spinach block in a colander, and run hot water over it. Allow spinach to thaw and drain; then press all of the water out of it. While spinach is thawing, melt margarine in a large skillet, and saute the onions until limp. Stir in the thoroughly drained spinach, and saute for 2 minutes. Spread spinach on bottom of skillet, and sprinkle with garlic powder, Worcestershire, and Tabasco; then salt to taste. Stir all remaining ingredients into spinach; blend well. Spray a combination baking and serving dish with spray-oil, and fill with the spinach mixture. Bake at 350 degrees for 25 to 30 minutes. Serve on crackers or with tortilla chips.

Green Chili Cheese Balls

1/2 cup margarine, softened	1 (4-oz.) can chopped green chilies
2 cups grated sharp Cheddar cheese	1 cup plain flour
1/2 teaspoon salt	

Preheat oven to 375 degrees. In an electric mixer, cream margarine with grated cheese and salt. Add green chilies and flour; mix until just barely blended. Form into quarter-size balls, and bake on a spray-oil prepared baking pan in the preheated oven for 12 to 15 minutes. These may be made in advance and frozen. If frozen, baking time is approximately 18 minutes.

Jerusalem Cheese-Puff Rolls

1 (17-1/4-oz.) package frozen puff pastry sheets, thawed	1/4 cup sour cream
1/4 cup cream cheese	1 cup grated Cheddar cheese
1/4 cup cottage cheese or ricotta cheese	1/4 teaspoon salt
	1 egg

Preheat oven to 350 degrees. Spray 2 cookie sheets with spray-oil, and lay a puff pastry sheet on each. In a medium bowl, combine all the remaining ingredients except the egg; and blend well. Place 1/2 of the mixture in the center of each pastry. Beat the egg, and brush the edges of the pastry with the egg. Lift the underside of the long side edges, and brush with egg. Pull the long side edges toward the top, and press together to seal very tightly; then roll downward to form a raised, rolled seal. Repeat with second pastry. Score the tops of the rolls with a knife using an "X" design. Bake in a preheated oven for about 30 to 35 minutes. Allow pastry to cool slightly before slicing. Present the entire golden pastry when serving; then slice to serve. The slices may be whole or cut into bite-size pieces.

Makes a beautiful and very appealing presentation, yet is so easy to prepare. It can also be served as a breakfast dish since it is light and very delicate. Add fresh fruit on the side when serving in the morning.

Baked Mushroom Turnovers

3 tablespoons margarine, melted	1 teaspoon salt
8 oz. fresh mushrooms, minced	1/4 teaspoon dried thyme
1 large onion, minced	4 tablespoons plain flour
1/4 cup sour cream	Wonton wrappers

Preheat oven to 375 degrees. In a large skillet, melt the margarine, and saute the mushrooms and onions until soft. Stir in the sour cream, salt, thyme, and flour; mix well. Place filling on 1/2 of a wonton; then fold over the other half. Seal the edges by moistening with water then pressing together; repeat until all filling is used. Prepare a cookie sheet with spray-oil. Place the filled wontons on the cookie sheet, and bake in the preheated oven for 10 minutes; then turn the wontons over, and cook an additional 5 minutes.

Buffalo Bites

2 lbs. boneless, skinless chicken breasts	1/2 cup Texas Pete, Trappey's Hot Sauce , or other red liquid hot sauce (do not use Tabasco sauce)
1/2 cup margarine, melted	Cornflakes, finely crushed

Cut chicken breasts into bite-size pieces, and place in a glass bowl. Melt the margarine, and add the red hot sauce; pour 1/2 of the sauce over the chicken pieces. Reserve the remaining 1/2 sauce for later. Toss chicken pieces to coat completely; set aside for 1/2 hour. Crush the cornflakes into fine crumbs, and place in bowl. Preheat oven to 350 degrees when ready to cook. Drain the chicken pieces, discarding the sauce; then roll in the crumbs. Place chicken pieces in a spray-oil prepared baking pan in a single layer. Bake in the preheated oven until done throughout and browned, about 15 to 18 minutes. Serve the Buffalo Bites warm with the reserved sauce, warmed for dipping, on the side.

London Broil With a Secret

The recipe may also be used as an entree served over hot white rice.

London broil	Salt
Margarine	Fresh, coarsely ground black
Soy sauce	pepper

Partially freeze the London broil to slice easily into thin slices. Use a nonstick skillet with a very small amount of melted margarine. Heat the skillet on high, and quickly brown the beef slices on both sides. This requires a very short amount of time since the beef should be kept on the rare side. (Do not overcook and make shoe leather!) Just before removing beef from the skillet, sprinkle both sides with soy sauce and a little salt. Taste for salt; then sprinkle moderately with the fresh, coarsely ground black pepper. Serve immediately.

The "secrets" to the recipe are the quick, high-temperature cooking method; the fresh, coarsely ground black pepper; the super-quick preparation; and the mingling of favors.

Confetti Bread

1 loaf frozen bread dough	4 oz. chopped green chilies,
1 lb. hot bulk sausage	drained
3 cups grated mozzarella cheese	1 egg white, lightly beaten
2 oz. chopped pimentos, drained	Parmesan cheese

Thaw the bread dough, and allow to rise according to package directions. On a floured board, roll out the dough with a rolling pin to 1/8-inch thickness. In a skillet, brown and crumble the sausage until it is done; drain. Sprinkle the cooked sausage and the cheese over the top surface of the rolled-out bread dough. Dot the surface of the cheese with tiny bits of the pimento and green chilies to give a confetti appearance. Roll dough like a jelly roll beginning on the long side of the dough; then brush the top with the egg white. Sprinkle with Parmesan cheese. Bake in a preheated oven according to bread dough package directions. Allow to cool slightly before slicing. Cut whole slices into quarters or smaller pieces.

Sherried Camembert Cheese

Make one day in advance.

	1/4 cup finely chopped pecans
1/2 lb. Camembert cheese	Unpeeled fresh red and green
1/4 lb. unsalted butter,	pears, washed and cut in
very soft	wedges
1/4 cup dry sherry	Wheat Thin crackers

Remove the rind from the Camembert cheese, and allow to soften to room temperature. In an electric mixer, cream the cheese and butter completely. Then, using a very low speed, slowly beat in the sherry, and continue to beat until the mixture is light. Cover the bowl, and refrigerate overnight. The next day, shape the cheese mixture into a ball, and roll in the chopped pecans. Refrigerate until firm; then slice the ball in half. Place the 2 halves side-by-side with the pecans facing upward on a flat serving platter. Place the pear wedges with colors alternating in a design around the cheese. Serve with a cheese spreader and additional Wheat Thin crackers.

Hot Shrimp Tarts

1 package refrigerated folded pie crusts 1-1/2 lbs. chopped, cooked shrimp 1/4 cup black olives, diced	1 teaspoon lemon juice 1/2 teaspoon salt 1/2 teaspoon horseradish 3 plus tablespoons mayonnaise

Unfold pie crusts, and allow to come to room temperature. Roll slightly thinner with a rolling pin; then cut 3-inch rounds from the pastry with a biscuit cutter. Roll each pastry round thinner, and set aside. Combine shrimp, black olives, lemon juice, salt, and horseradish until mixed. Add just enough mayonnaise to hold the mixture together. Fill 1/2 of each pastry round with the shrimp mixture; then fold other half of the pastry over filling. Crimp the two edges of the tart with a salad fork to seal and give a fluted appearance; repeat with all pastry rounds. Place tarts on a cookie sheet sprayed with spray-oil. When ready to bake preheat the oven to 375 degrees. Bake for 12 minutes on a mid-level oven rack; then move pan to a top oven rack for 4 minutes or until lightly browned. Serve hot. Makes 25.

French Francs

6 oz. sharp Cheddar cheese, grated 3 oz. Roquefort cheese (bleu cheese may be substituted) 1 cup margarine, softened	1-1/2 teaspoons seasoning salt 2-3/4 cups plain flour Dash cayenne pepper 1 cup pecans, chopped

In a food processor or electric mixer, combine the Cheddar cheese and Roquefort cheese until blended. Add the margarine, seasoning salt, flour, and cayenne pepper; blend to mix. Then mix in the pecans. Place the dough on waxed paper, and roll into a long roll about the diameter of a silver dollar. Wrap the roll in waxed paper, and refrigerate for 2 hours. Preheat oven to 375 degrees. Using an electric knife, slice the chilled roll into thin slices or "francs." Bake on an ungreased cookie sheet for 10 minutes or until lightly browned. Makes 36.

Microwave Potato Skin Boats

3 medium Idaho potatoes, scrubbed clean	4 green onions, thinly sliced with tops
1/4 cup margarine	2 tablespoons chopped green chilies
1/2 teaspoon dill weed	1 oz. black olives, chopped
1/4 teaspoon salt	1/3 cup cooked, crumbled, real bacon bits (no imitation)
1/4 teaspoon Tabasco sauce	
3 oz. sharp Cheddar cheese, grated	

Pierce potatoes, and cook in a microwave-safe covered dish on full power for 8 to 9 minutes. Cool potatoes enough to handle. Cut potatoes lengthwise into halves; then carefully scoop out the potato while leaving 1/4-inch of the potato on the skins. Cut the halves in half lengthwise to make "boats." In a small saucepan, melt margarine; add dill weed, salt, and Tabasco. Brush both sides of potato skin boats with the mixture. Place boats on paper plates with the potato skin sides upward, and microwave on full power for 4 minutes. Turn boats over, and microwave on full power an additional 3 minutes. Watch the boats as they cook the second time to keep from over or under cooking. Because of potato skin thickness and differences in microwave wattages, this time may vary. Boats should be slightly crispy after they cool. In a small bowl, mix all of the remaining ingredients. Fill the boats with the mixture, and bake in the oven at 350 degrees, or microwave on high until the mixture is bubbly. Makes 12 boats.

Teriyaki Steak Appetizers

The beef should marinate for 24 hours, but tastes good even if marinated for a shorter time.

1-1/2 lbs. flank steak
1/4 cup soy sauce
1-1/4 teaspoons ground ginger

2 teaspoons vinegar
1/2 cup vegetable oil
1-1/2 teaspoons garlic powder
1 tablespoon honey

Place flank steak in a glass dish just large enough to fit flat. Mix all remaining ingredients, and beat well to completely blend. Pour marinade over the steak; allow to sit for 2 minutes; then turn the steak. Cover and refrigerate; turn steak several times to evenly marinate. Grill on a medium-hot grill for 5 minutes per side. The steak can be served medium rare, if desired. Slice steak thin with the grain; then cut into bite-size pieces.

Dilled Carrot Sticks

Refrigerate overnight.

8 small carrots, scraped and trimmed
1 cup dill pickle juice

1 tablespoon dill weed
1 tablespoon fresh chopped chives
Sour cream (optional)

Cut carrots into quarters; then cut quarters in half. Place the carrots into a medium saucepan with the pickle juice, and bring to a boil. Reduce heat to a simmer, and cook carrots until just tender-crisp. Remove from heat; pour carrots and juice into a heat-safe plastic bowl with a lid. Refrigerate overnight. At serving time, drain carrots; then toss with the dill weed and chives. A small bowl of sour cream can be served beside the carrots for dipping, if desired.

Toasted Mushroom Triangles

1/2 lb. fresh mushrooms, washed, dried, and finely chopped	3 teaspoons horseradish
	1/4 teaspoon garlic powder
	1/2 cup toasted almonds, chopped
2 tablespoons margarine, melted	Loaf of white sandwich bread
3 oz. cream cheese, softened	White wooden round toothpicks
1 (10-3/4-oz.) can cream of chicken soup	Additional melted margarine for tops
2 teaspoons Worcestershire sauce	Paprika

Preheat oven to 450 degrees. In a skillet, saute mushrooms in the margarine; then drain and set aside. In an electric mixer, beat cream cheese, soup, Worcestershire sauce, horseradish, and garlic powder until smooth. By hand, stir in the mushrooms and almonds; set aside. Trim crusts from bread slices; then roll each slice with a rolling pin to flatten. Place 1 tablespoon of the mushroom mixture diagonally across the bread. Bring opposite corners of the bread together to overlap in the center; secure with a toothpick. Place triangles on ungreased cookie sheet. Brush tops with melted margarine, and sprinkle with paprika. Bake in the preheated oven for about 7 minutes or until browned and warm. Select the oven rack level that best suits the oven being used; watch carefully. Do not overbake.

The triangles can be made as much as 24 hours ahead of time and refrigerated covered. Allow to stand unrefrigerated for about 15 to 20 minutes while the oven preheats. They may also be made and frozen; store in a tight container. Thaw before baking.

At parties these triangles are magic; they disappear before your very eyes. My cousin, Diane Pfeiffer Presley, has fabulous appetizer recipes and is always so very gracious about sharing them with me and you. I will have to take a tiny amount of credit for her interest in the culinary arts since she would visit me in the summers, and we would make goodies. She and her recipes are more than special as everyone who knows her would agree!

Party Fruit Tart

The crust can be made several hours before assembly and kept in a closed oven to stay crisp. Make the cream cheese mixture and the lemon mixture at the same time, and refrigerate both. Assemble the tart one hour before serving.

1 package refrigerated crescent rolls
8 oz. cream cheese
8 oz. whipped topping

1/2 cup granulated sugar
1 tablespoon cornstarch
1/2 cup orange juice
2 tablespoons lemon juice
1/4 cup water
Dash of salt
1 (11-oz.) can mandarin oranges, well drained
1 fresh kiwi berry, peeled and sliced
1 pint fresh strawberries, washed and sliced

Preheat oven to 350 degrees. Open the crescent roll package, unroll dough, and allow to come to room temperature. Prepare a 9- x 13-inch cookie pan with spray-oil. Press the dough seams to form a solid sheet. Stretch and roll the dough until it fits flat in the bottom of the pan. Bake in the preheated oven for 10 to 14 minutes. Crust should be browned and crispy; allow to cool completely. In an electric mixer, combine cream cheese and whipped topping until smooth. Spread cream cheese mixture on cooled crust. In a small saucepan, combine sugar and cornstarch until blended; then gradually stir in the orange juice, keeping the mixture smooth. Add lemon juice, water, and salt; bring to a boil, and allow to boil for 1 minute. Remove sauce from heat, and refrigerate to cool completely. While sauce is cooling, arrange the fruit in a pleasing design on the cream cheese mixture. Pour the cooled sauce over the fruit; cover and refrigerate until serving time. Serve cold, cut in squares.

This is absolutely beautiful. The color combination is luscious. It's almost too pretty to cut. But stand back when it is served; it tastes even better than it looks!

The Very Best Guacamole Dip

2 ripe avocados
1/2 medium sweet or mild
   onion
2 cloves garlic
Juice of one fresh lemon
2 medium tomatoes, diced fine

1/2 teaspoon garlic salt
1/2 teaspoon onion salt
1/2 teaspoon freshly ground
   black pepper
Tabasco sauce to taste

Peel avocados, split, and discard pits; then slice. In a food processor or blender, finely cut the onion and garlic, do not puree. Remove the onion mixture to a large bowl; set aside. Place the avocado slices in the food processor or blender, puree the avocados with the lemon juice until smooth consistency. Put avocado mixture into the bowl with the onion mixture, and add the tomato; mix well. Add the remaining 4 ingredients, and blend well. Cover the bowl, and refrigerate for at least 30 minutes to allow flavors to blend. Serve with tortilla chips. Can also be used as a salad topping over shredded lettuce.

Our friend Wayne Thompson, whom my husband, Joe, and I sponsored as a Canadian Officer when he was stationed at Maxwell AFB for the Air War College, gave me this recipe. I titled it, since he had modestly named it only "Guacamole Dip." Upon his return to Ottawa, Canada, he was assigned to be chief flying officer for the Prime Minister and the Queen, if she was "in town!" Talented guy and charming too, not to mention his beautiful wife, Vickie, and their eight great children.

Baked Gouda en Croute

1 package refrigerated crescent rolls	1/2 teaspoon Cavender's All Purpose Greek Seasoning, divided
1 Gouda cheese round	

Preheat the oven to recommended temperature on the crescent roll package. Using a spray-oil prepared baking pan, unroll the crescent rolls, and divide into 2 portions. Press all the seams together to form a solid sheet for each portion. Remove the wrapper from the Gouda cheese, and slice the whole cheese, horizontally, into 2 thinner rounds. Place a round of cheese in the center of each crescent roll sheet, and sprinkle with half of the Greek Seasoning on each cheese. Fold the dough to completely and tightly enclose the cheese. Bake in the preheated oven for the recommended time on the package; then continue to bake, watching carefully, until the rolls are browned and cheese is melted inside. This time may vary with each making. Allow the baked Goudas to cool slightly before cutting into thin wedges. The wedges may also be cut into bite-size pieces. Serve warm.

South of the Border Crackers

1 (14-1/2-oz.) box Cheez-It crackers	1 tablespoon Worcestershire sauce
1/2 cup margarine, melted	1/2 teaspoon seasoning salt
1 (1-1/4-oz.) package dry taco seasoning mix	

Preheat oven to 250 degrees. Place the crackers in a 9- x 13-inch baking dish. In a bowl, mix all remaining ingredients, and pour over the crackers. Stir well to season the crackers. Bake in the preheated oven for 1 hour; stir about every 15 minutes. After cooking time, pour onto waxed paper, and spread crackers to cool. Store in airtight container when completely cooled. Makes 6 cups.

Cheese Crispies Supreme

1 cup margarine, softened (do not use light margarine) 2 cups plain flour	2 cups finely grated sharp Cheddar cheese 2 cups Rice Krispies

Preheat oven to 325 degrees. In an electric mixer, combine the softened margarine, flour, and finely grated cheese until well blended. Add the Rice Krispies, and mix until barely blended. Form into logs the diameter of a quarter; then roll in waxed paper, and chill in the refrigerator. When ready to bake, pinch off by pieces, and flatten tops with a salad fork to give a slightly grooved design. Bake on an ungreased cookie sheet in the preheated oven for 15 to 18 minutes or until firmly set and lightly browned on the bottom. Do not brown tops. Makes 100.

Elizabeth Hall, or "Beanie," makes these excellent cheese crispies for gifts. And welcome ones they are in our busy world where "homemade goodies" are getting to be rare treats these days. The baked cheese crispies freeze very well and also make great traveling snacks. "Beanie" and her husband, Warren, have been steadfast friends and mentors for most of my life, and that is even better than "homemade goodies!"

Italian Appetizer Rolls

1 package frozen Parker House Rolls	1/2 lb. pepperoni, thinly sliced 1/2 lb. Swiss cheese, cubed

Thaw frozen rolls. Prepare a cookie sheet with spray-oil. When rolls are thawed, place 2 or 3 pepperoni slices and a cube of Swiss cheese on a roll. Form the dough to fit around the cheese and pepperoni; then roll to form a ball, and place on the cookie sheet. Repeat the process until all the rolls are made. Preheat the oven to 350 degrees, and bake for about 20 minutes or until cheese is melted and rolls are lightly browned.

Summertime White Pizza Squares

2 packages refrigerated
   crescent rolls
2 (8-oz.) packages cream cheese,
   softened
2/3 cup mayonnaise
1 teaspoon dill weed
1 pint cherry tomatoes,
   quartered

1 cup pitted black olives,
   drained and sliced
1/2 green pepper, diced
1/2 sweet red pepper, diced
2 oz. pepperoni, diced
Anchovies; whole, strips, or
   minced (optional)

Prepare a large cookie sheet with spray-oil. On the cookie sheet, roll out both packages of the crescent rolls. Press all seams together to form a solid crust covering the pan. Preheat oven, and cook crust according to package directions; allow to cool completely. In a bowl, mix cream cheese, mayonnaise, and dill weed until very well blended. When crust has cooled, spread the cream cheese mixture over the entire top. Place the cherry tomato quarters in an attractive design over the entire top; add black olive slices between the tomatoes. Sprinkle evenly the diced green peppers, red peppers, and pepperoni. Place anchovies on last, if desired. Refrigerate to set; then cut into small squares to serve cold.

Debby's Mardi Gras Squares

1/2 cup margarine	2 cups grated sharp Cheddar
1 medium onion, chopped	cheese
1 (10-oz.) package frozen	4 eggs, well beaten
chopped broccoli, thawed	1 (9-oz.) package Jiffy corn
4 oz. chopped pimento	bread mix

Preheat oven to 350 degrees. In a skillet, melt the margarine, and saute the onions until soft. Add all the remaining ingredients including the uncooked broccoli, and blend. Prepare a 9- x 13-inch baking dish with spray-oil; then pour in the mixture. Bake for 45 minutes. Cut into bite-size squares. Serve warm or room temperature.

This may also be made in two 8-inch round cake pans and cut into wedges. It may be made ahead of time and frozen before cutting. If frozen, allow to thaw; then wrap in aluminum foil to heat until piping hot.

Sesame Drums

Marinate for 4 hours.	1/3 cup Kikkoman Teriyaki
	Baste & Glaze
18 chicken wing drumettes	1 large clove garlic, minced
1 tablespoon soy sauce	1 tablespoon chopped chives
1 tablespoon dry sherry	2 teaspoons toasted sesame
	seeds

Wash and pat dry the drumettes. In a glass bowl, mix all ingredients except drumettes and sesame seeds. Place drumettes in marinade, and turn to coat; cover and refrigerate for 4 hours. Turn drumettes several times. When ready to cook, remove the drumettes from marinade to a plate, and sprinkle with sesame seeds. Place drumettes on a grill with medium-low heat. Cook slowly with grill cover down. Turn several times during grilling. Before removing the drumettes from the grill, check the chicken to be sure it is done throughout. Makes 18.

Diane's Artichoke Bacon Dip with Pecans

Make several hours or overnight in advance.

1 (14-oz.) can artichoke hearts, well drained
8 bacon slices, cooked crisp and crumbled

1-1/2 teaspoons Worcestershire sauce
3/4 cup mayonnaise
1-1/2 teaspoons lemon juice
1/2 small onion, finely chopped
1/2 cup chopped pecans

In a glass bowl, chop the drained artichoke hearts; then stir in all the remaining ingredients until mixed. Cover and refrigerate for several hours to allow flavors to blend. Serve cold with crackers.

Das-a-Gouda Dip

1 (10-oz.) round Gouda cheese, with red wax covering removed
1/2 cup sour cream

1 tablespoon dry Italian salad dressing mix
Red tip lettuce leaves
Paprika

Carefully scoop out center of the cheese, leaving 1/4-inch shell intact. Set shell aside. In a food processor, blend the scooped-out cheese with the sour cream and dry salad dressing mix; blend well. Spoon the cheese mixture into the Gouda shell. Sprinkle with paprika. Place lettuce leaves around serving platter. Serve chilled with crackers. Makes 1 cup of spread.

Tennessee Temptation

1 round loaf French, Italian, or sour dough bread	1/2 cup chopped cooked ham
4 oz. grated Monterey Jack cheese with jalapenos	1 (4.5-oz.) can chopped green chilies, undrained
4 oz. grated Cheddar cheese	1/3 cup finely chopped onion
8 ozs. cream cheese, softened	1/4 teaspoon Worcestershire sauce
1-1/2 cups sour cream	Crackers or chips for dipping

To prepare the bread, use a serrated edged knife, and cut a thin slice from the top to use later as a lid. Hollow-out the center of the bread. Cutting around the circle, leave enough bread to make a sturdy "bowl" to fill. Lift the center of bread out whole; slice and set aside. In a bowl, mix all remaining ingredients; then fill the bread "bowl," placing the bread "lid" on top; wrap in aluminum foil. Place the foil-wrapped package on a cookie sheet and surround with extra bread slices. Bake at 350 degrees until extra bread slices are toasted; remove them from the oven, and continue to cook the foil package. It should bake for a total of 1 hour. To serve, remove the foil, and place on a serving platter. Break the toasted bread slices into dipping pieces, and place around the bread "bowl." Have additional crackers or chips for dipping, and eventually eat the "bowl."

Joann Young gave this recipe to my mother, along with many, many others. She is a superb cook, and she and her husband, George, love to entertain. Definitely do not turn down a meal at their place!

Bambini

1 cup ricotta	1 (10-oz.) package large flaky
1/2 cup grated mozzarella	refrigerator biscuits
cheese	40 thin slices pepperoni
1/4 cup freshly grated Parmesan	Garlic salt to taste
cheese	

Preheat oven to 350 degrees. In a bowl, combine the ricotta, mozzarella, and Parmesan cheeses, and mix. Open the biscuit tube, and divide dough into biscuits. Cut each biscuit horizontally in half to make 20 pieces. Gently shape the halves into ovals about 2-1/2- x 4 inches. Place 2 slices of pepperoni off center on the dough; then top with 1 tablespoon of cheese mixture, and sprinkle with a dash of garlic salt. Repeat with all of the dough. Moisten the edges with a little water; then fold dough over filling, and pinch edges to seal; repeat with all of the dough. Place the bambini on a spray-oil prepared cookie sheet, and bake in the preheated oven for 20 minutes or until browned. Serve warm. Makes 20.

Gary's Tart Cocktail Sausages

1/4 cup margarine	1 large clove garlic, crushed
1/4 cup lemon juice	1/2 large onion, minced
1/4 cup vinegar	1 package cooked cocktail
1/4 cup Worcestershire sauce	sausages, cut in halves
1/4 cup catsup	

In a saucepan, combine all the ingredients except the cocktail sausages. Bring sauce to a boil; then reduce heat, and simmer. Simmer the sauce, uncovered, for 20 minutes. Add the already cooked cocktail sausages to the sauce, and simmer for 10 minutes. Pour into a chafing dish or other warming-type container to keep warm while serving.

Gary Clements, my son by marriage, loves these tart, tasty morsels. So do I!

Sesame Toasties

1 long French baguette loaf 1/2 cup melted margarine, more if needed	Sesame seeds Garlic or onion salt Paprika

Preheat oven to 250 degrees. Slice the entire baguette into thin, round slices. Place slices in a single layer on an ungreased baking pan. Brush both sides of the bread with melted margarine. Sprinkle the top with a few sesame seeds, garlic or onion salt, and paprika. Place pan in the preheated oven; then turn the heat off. Keep the oven door closed, and allow the toasties to remain in the oven for 8 to 24 hours. Store in an airtight container.

These Sesame Toasties are very versatile. They may be served by themselves as an appetizer, like crackers, with soups or salads, or with most any appetizer spread.

Golden Nuggets

4 oz. Cheddar cheese, finely
   grated
2 tablespoons margarine,
   softened
	1/2 cup plain flour
	1/2 teaspoon paprika
	2 tablespoons water
	1 lb. cooked ham

Preheat oven to 400 degrees. In a food processor or blender, combine the cheese, margarine, flour, paprika, and water; blend into a soft dough. Cut the ham into 1-inch cubes, approximately 20. Make a small ball of the dough, flatten with palm of hand, and shape completely around the ham cube; repeat for all ham cubes. Place nuggets on a spray-oil prepared cookie sheet. Bake in the preheated oven for 15 minutes or until light golden brown. Serve hot or cold. Makes 20.

Bob Cheers' Smoked Salmon Spread

8 oz. whipped cream cheese	2 teaspoons lemon juice
1/4 lb. smoked salmon, flaked	1/4 teaspoon garlic powder
2 tablespoons minced green onion	1/2 teaspoon Tabasco sauce
1/2 teaspoon dried dill weed	1/4 teaspoon Worcestershire sauce

Using a glass bowl, mix all ingredients until well blended. Cover the bowl, and refrigerate for 30 minutes to allow flavors to blend.

You also may want to try this recipe with smoked trout or other cooked or smoked fish.

Bob Cheers is the epitome of the rugged outdoorsman. He fishes for salmon in Michigan and smokes it himself; hunts elk in Montana for a month at a time and knows how to cook it; telemark skis; canoes; owns a great backpacking and bicycling shop; leads the Boy Scouts; is a loving husband to our very special friend and pretty lady, Alice, and a business partner and father to two great sons and their families. Wow, Bob, with an "intro" like that you ought to put me in your will! He does make this grand spread with his own caught and smoked salmon on our family ski trips together.

Jalapeno Wontons

1 lb. Monterey Jack cheese, grated	1 (4-oz.) can chopped green chilies
1/3 cup jalapeno pepper slices, chopped	1 package wonton wrappers
	Vegetable oil

Take care to fully seal these delicious morsels before frying. In a food processor or blender, combine the grated cheese, jalapeno peppers, and green chilies until well blended. Place 1 teaspoon of cheese mixture on a wonton wrapper; fold into a triangle. Moisten edges of triangle, and press edges to seal. Repeat until all cheese mixture is used. Place wontons on a pan; then place pan in freezer for a short period of time to allow to chill; do not freeze solid. When chilled, fry the wontons in oil until golden, and drain on paper towels. Sprinkle lightly with salt. Serve plain or with guacamole as a dip. Makes 50.

Cajun Fingers

1 lb. boneless, skinless chicken breasts, partially frozen	1/4 teaspoon onion salt
Garlic salt, to sprinkle chicken	1/4 teaspoon cayenne pepper
1/2 teaspoon garlic powder	1/2 cup plain flour
1/4 teaspoon garlic salt	Vegetable oil

Dipping Sauce:	1/4 cup Texas Pete, Trappey's
1/4 cup margarine, melted	Hot Sauce, or other red liquid hot sauce (do not use Tabasco)

Cut partially frozen chicken breasts into strips, and sprinkle with garlic salt. Set aside for 30 minutes. In a bowl, combine all remaining ingredients except oil, and blend well. Dredge chicken strips in the seasoned flour to coat. In a skillet, heat oil to hot, but not smoking. Fry chicken strips until completely done, being careful not to undercook or overcook. Drain on paper towel. To make sauce, combine margarine and hot sauce; stir to blend. Serve chicken hot or warm with the warm dipping sauce on the side.

Beth's Hanky Pankies

1 lb. lean ground beef
1 lb. light, hot sausage
1 teaspoon oregano
1 teaspoon black pepper

1 lb. Velveeta cheese, cut into
  chunks
8 whole English muffins, split
  in halves

In a nonstick skillet or pot, cook the ground beef and sausage together; drain well. Stir in the oregano and pepper until mixed. Add the cheese; mix and simmer until cheese is completely melted and blended. Spread the hot mixture on the English muffin halves, and cut into quarters with a pizza cutter or a sharp knife. Bake on a cookie sheet at 425 degrees for 8 to 10 minutes.

These may also be frozen before baking. Place quarters on cookie sheets, and freeze; uncovered. As soon as they are frozen solid remove to a Ziplock bag, and store in freezer. When cooking the frozen quarters, do not thaw; just place on a cookie sheet. Bring oven temperature to broil. Bake on the bottom rack for 5 minutes; then move to top rack for 3 minutes. Watch carefully to keep from over-browning. Makes 64 appetizers.

My husband's cousin, Beth Fulghom, sent me this recipe. She is a great cook, hostess, mother, wife, daughter, sweet relative, and friend. You will enjoy a number of her excellent recipes throughout my cookbooks. Her comment on this one was, "Joe'll love these!" We ALL do!

Russian Stroganoff

1 lb. lean ground round	1/4 teaspoon freshly ground
1/4 cup margarine, melted	black pepper
1/2 cup chopped onion	1 (10-3/4-oz.) can cream of
8 oz. fresh mushrooms, washed	chicken soup
and chopped	1/4 cup chopped fresh parsley
1 clove garlic, minced	2 tablespoons A-1 sauce
2 tablespoons plain flour	1 cup sour cream
2 teaspoons salt	

In a large skillet, brown the ground beef, and drain; set aside. Melt margarine, and saute the onions, mushrooms, and garlic. Stir in the beef and the remaining ingredients except the sour cream. Allow mixture to simmer for 20 minutes. While mixture is hot but NOT boiling, stir in the sour cream. Never allow stroganoff to come to a boil after adding sour cream. Pour into a chafing dish or other warming-type dish, and keep hot to serve. Just before serving, top with a colorful garnish. Serve with small toasted slices of French bread.

Greek Isles Tart

2 tablespoons chopped black	1 small clove garlic, minced and
olives	crushed
2 tablespoons chopped roasted,	11 oz. feta or goat cheese,
sweet red pepper	crumbled
1/2 teaspoon olive oil	11 oz. cream cheese, softened
	3 eggs , well beaten

Place all ingredients into a food processor or blender, and blend until well mixed. Select an 8-inch fluted-edge tart pan or attractive pie plate, and spray with spray-oil. Spoon the mixture in the pan, and bake at 325 degrees for 45 minutes or until firm and a knife blade comes out clean when inserted in the center of the tart. Serve with small French bread slices, toasted or untoasted.

A very pungent appetizer and is best eaten with plain bread.

Dear's "Fancy" Sardine Spread

Make several hours in advance.	1 teaspoon prepared mustard
1 (3-3/4-oz.) can sardines	1/2 teaspoon Worcestershire
1 tablespoon minced onion	sauce
3 tablespoons mayonnaise	3/4 teaspoon soy sauce
1 teaspoon lemon juice	1/2 teaspoon paprika
1 teaspoon Durkee's Famous	1/4 teaspoon salt
Sauce	1/4 teaspoon Tabasco sauce

Lift sardines from oil, and place into a medium glass bowl. Split sardines in half; remove and discard bones. Mash sardines; then add remaining ingredients. Mix until completely blended. Cover and refrigerate for several hours to allow flavors to blend. Serve on hard crackers.

This was my grandmother's recipe when I was a child. Back in those ancient days, sardines were considered "gourmet." Well, actually, I don't recall the word "gourmet" being used. The word in those days was "fancy." My grandfather loved to shop in the only store in Montgomery, Alabama, that carried "fancy" foods. He didn't cook, but he always had a pantry stuffed with these specialty foods.

Pancho's Pinwheels

Refrigerate 2 hours before serving.	6 slices bacon, cooked and
2 (8-oz.) packages cream	crumbled
cheese, softened	1/2 cup diced sweet red pepper
1/2 cup mayonnaise	1/2 cup diced celery
1 (1-oz.) package Hidden Valley	1/3 cup black olives, drained
Ranch dressing mix	and sliced
3 green onions, chopped	4 to 5 medium flour tortillas
with tops	

In a bowl, mix all ingredients except tortillas until well blended. Spread mixture on tortillas evenly. Roll tortillas tight, and wrap tightly in waxed paper. Refrigerate for 2 hours or overnight. Cut each roll diagonally into bite-size slices. Makes about 36 appetizers.

Godbold's Texas Spread

1 (10-1/2-oz.) can jalapeno-flavored bean dip	8 oz. grated Monterey Jack cheese with jalapeno peppers
1 refrigerated carton guacamole dip	1 large fresh tomato, diced
8 oz. sour cream	3 green onions, sliced thin with tops
1 (1-1/4-oz.) package dry taco mix	1 cup black olives, quartered
	Tortilla chips

On a flat platter, make layers of the ingredients. Spread the bean dip as a base; then spread the guacamole on beans. Mix the sour cream with the dry taco mix until blended, and spread over the guacamole layer. Sprinkle the grated cheese over the entire surface. Mix the tomatoes, onions, and olives; then sprinkle over the cheese layer. Serve at room temperature with tortilla chips. May be made in advance, covered, and refrigerated until serving time.

Florida Antipasto

Marinate overnight. Also makes a beautiful salad on lettuce.	1 head fresh cauliflower, washed
1 package Good Seasons Italian salad dressing mix, prepared	1 (14-oz.) can artichoke hearts, drained and quartered
3 oz. bleu cheese, crumbled	2 (6-oz.) cans button mushrooms, drained
1 head fresh broccoli, washed	1 medium-size jar stuffed green olives, drained

Make the salad dressing according to the package directions. Pour the dressing into a large bowl, and add the bleu cheese crumbles. Mash the cheese, and mix to blend. Cut broccoli and cauliflower florets into bite-size pieces; discard stems. Add all remaining ingredients to the salad dressing. Toss several times to coat vegetables with the dressing. Cover and refrigerate overnight. Serve cold in a beautiful crystal or glass bowl. Have toothpicks for skewering.

Half-Baked Pizzas!

6 English muffins, split (I prefer Bay's, if available)
1 large avocado
1 tablespoon lemon juice
Salt
Black Bean Spread (see below)
2 cups shredded Monterey Jack cheese with jalapeno peppers
1 sweet red pepper, chopped fine
1 yellow pepper, chopped fine
1 green pepper, chopped fine
10 green onions, chopped with tops
12 jumbo pitted black olives, chopped
Crushed red pepper flakes (optional)
Sour cream

Black Bean Spread:

1 (15-oz.) can black beans, drained
4 cloves garlic, peeled
2 to 4 drops Tabasco sauce
1 cup chopped fresh tomatoes

Preheat oven to 450 degrees. Using a cookie sheet, bake muffin halves in preheated oven until crisp, watching carefully, for about 5 minutes. Immediately remove muffins from oven; set aside to cool. Peel and seed the avocado. Slice thin slices into a small bowl; then sprinkle with lemon juice and salt to taste. Toss very gently, and set aside. To make Black Bean Spread, in a food processor or blender, puree the beans, garlic, and Tabasco. Remove the bean mixture to a bowl, and stir in the chopped tomatoes. Evenly spread the Black Bean Spread over each cooled muffin half. Sprinkle with Monterey Jack cheese. In a small bowl, mix all peppers, onions, and olives. Spoon on top of cheese. Top each with a few slices of avocado. Sprinkle with a tiny pinch of crushed red pepper flakes, if desired. Bake at 450 degrees about 10 minutes or until cheese is bubbly. Cut with a pizza cutter into quarters, and add a tiny dollop of sour cream to each quarter.

These can also be served whole as individual pizzas. Makes 12 pizzas or 48 appetizers.

Beverages

Southern Slush Punch

Make early in the day or the night before serving to allow the punch to freeze.

2 cups prepared tea
1 (6-oz.) can frozen orange
   juice, thawed

1 (12-oz.) can frozen lemonade,
   thawed
1 cup granulated sugar
2 cups bourbon
6 cups water

Mix all ingredients until the sugar is completely dissolved. Pour into a plastic container, and place in the freezer. Stir occasionally until punch is frozen. Remove punch from freezer 30 minutes before serving time. Serve the slush with a ladle.

You'll have to be careful with this one. One too many cups will render your tongue incapable of saying "Southern Slush Punch!" Shurrr does tasteee goood though!

Officer's Graduation Punch

1 bottle champagne, well chilled
1 quart ginger ale, well chilled

3/4 cup apricot brandy
3/4 cup vodka

Slowly pour all ingredients into a punch bowl. Add ice rings to chill. Additional ginger ale may be added for a lighter taste on a hot day. Serves 12.

coffees of the world

All coffee in the recipes below should be sweetened to taste, if desired. All whipped cream should be sweetened.

Cafe Au Lait: Half coffee, half hot milk, whipped cream

Cafe Parisian: Coffee, cognac, whipped cream

Caribbean Coffee: Coffee, rum, whipped cream, grated nutmeg

Mexican Coffee: Coffee, Kahlua, cinnamon stick, whipped cream, grated chocolate

Cafe Viennese: Coffee, cognac, whipped cream, grated nutmeg

Brazilian Coffee: Coffee, creme de cacao, cinnamon stick, whipped cream, grated chocolate

Cafe Martinique: Coffee, rum, cinnamon sticks, whipped cream, grated nutmeg

Tuscano Coffee: Coffee, brandy, lemon zest

For an interesting gathering, have a "Coffees of the World Party." Make GOOD coffee in copious amounts. Please no instant; my husband, Joe, would expire! Then set your coffee cart with all of the ingredients used in the coffees above. Select your prettiest china coffee cups that match, or make an assortment of pretty cup-and-saucer sets using the around the world theme, or use the same theme with interesting coffee mugs. Print a coffee menu for all of your guests to make their own coffees. Or better yet, present them all with a copy of this cookbook as a gift and tell them to turn to this page! What a gracious and generous hostess you would be both to your guests and to me!

Summer Breeze

1 (6-oz.) can frozen lemonade, undiluted 4 cups freshly brewed strong tea	1 quart ginger ale Cranberry juice

Thaw lemonade; then combine all ingredients except the cranberry juice until well mixed. Stir in enough cranberry juice to make the punch a pleasing color. Serve chilled as a punch using ice rings, or serve as a beverage in tall glasses filled with ice.

Melody's Late Night Smoothie

1/2 oz. coffee liqueur (more, if desired)	2 oz. Irish Creame Liqueur 3 scoops vanilla ice cream

Place all ingredients into blender or food processor, and blend. Pour into pretty, small wine glasses to serve.

Juliet's Jumpin' Juice

Ice Orange juice 3 to 4 oz. vodka	1/2 of an individual Tropical Passions, Strawberry Kiwi Crystal Light

Fill the blender container with ice. Pour orange juice to 1/2-inch below the top of the ice. Add vodka and Crystal Light granules; blend.

Poinsettia

1 bottle champagne Cranberry juice to taste	Small twist of lemon or lime per glass Sprig of fresh mint, if available

This can be made by the glass or in a punch bowl.

Mocha Ice Cream Punch

This can be partially made one day in advance.

4 tablespoons instant coffee
4 cups boiling water
Granulated sugar to taste

2 pints whipping cream, unwhipped
1/2 gallon vanilla or chocolate ice cream
1 quart club soda

Add the instant coffee to the boiling water, and sweeten with the sugar to taste. Allow coffee to cool; then stir in the unwhipped cream. This mixture can be made and refrigerated overnight, if desired. Thirty minutes before serving, place the ice cream into a punch bowl, and add the coffee mixture. Just before serving, slowly add the club soda to the punch. Stir gently to mix.

Cranberry Frappe

The recipe is measured in parts to allow the making of large or small amounts to suit your needs.

3 parts cranberry juice
2 parts pineapple juice

1 part lemon juice
Granulated sugar to taste
Ginger ale

Mix all ingredients except ginger ale, and freeze in ice cube trays or in plastic containers. Shortly before serving, remove frozen mixture from the freezer, and allow to slightly soften. Break into smaller pieces, and place in a blender. Add ginger ale in small amounts until a slush consistency is achieved. Serve in champagne glasses.

If the frappe mixture is frozen in ice cube trays, the cubes may be removed to a ziplock bag for storage.

Sparkling Cranberry Punch

Chilled cranberry juice	Chilled Sprite soda

Mix equal parts of cranberry juice with Sprite. Chill to serve. Cranapple or Crangrape juice may be substituted for the cranberry juice, if desired.

A perfect color for Christmas or Valentine's Day.

Perfectly Pink Punch

Lemonade mix	Chilled cranberry juice

Mix lemonade according to package directions, and chill; then mix in enough cranberry juice to suit your taste and color fancy. Chill to serve.

Both of the above punches are simple to make, light, and not overly sweet. Enjoy their flavors!

Spiced Apple Cider

1/2 gallon apple cider	2 cinnamon sticks
2 cups orange juice	5 whole cloves
3/4 cup lemon juice	1-1/2 teaspoons butter
1/4 cup honey	1/4 teaspoon allspice

In a Dutch oven, combine all ingredients, and bring to a boil. Cover and reduce heat to simmer for 1 hour. Strain before serving; serve hot. Makes 3 quarts.

Mocha Winter Warmer

1/2 cup unsweetened cocoa	3 cups milk
3 tablespoons instant coffee	2 cups water
1/4 cup granulated sugar	

In a medium saucepan, stir together the cocoa, instant coffee, and sugar. Gradually stir in the milk, taking care to dissolve the sugar; then add the water. Stir and heat over low heat until hot; do not allow to boil. Serve hot.

This can be made less rich and less fattening by using skim milk. It can be made richer by using Half and Half or cream substituted for the milk. Your choice for the occasion.

Homemade Kahlua

Make one MONTH in advance.

1 (2-oz.) jar instant coffee	2 cups water
2 cups brandy (use inexpensive brand)	2 cups granulated sugar
	1 vanilla bean

Use a glass jar with a screw-on lid. Combine all of the ingredients; then put lid on tightly, and shake. Shake once a week for 1 month before sampling and serving. Keep refrigerated the entire preparation time and while storing.

Makes a great topping for vanilla, chocolate, or coffee ice cream. It also makes a lovely gift when poured into small, pretty-shaped bottles.

Kahlua Kooler

1-1/2 generous scoops vanilla ice cream	1-1/2 oz. Kahlua

Place both ingredients into a blender to mix. After blending, pour into a wine glass, and serve with a spoon or a small straw. Serves 1.

Stories from the Victorian Verandah

O ur lives include an interweaving of memorable stories, often told on the broad verandah of an old Victorian home. We hope you'll be entertained and enjoy these vignettes.

"The Big House"

The charming watercolor of the large Victorian house on the front cover of this cookbook is of the Ellis Family's ancestral home, 8 miles from Fort Deposit, Alabama. The surrounding, rolling, green farmland was originally purchased in 1853 by Fielding Lewis and Elizabeth Jarvis Ellis. Construction on "The Big House" began about 1910, with the lumber being hauled in on mule wagons. Hence Ellis, original partner in Priester's Pecan Company, helped his parents, John Gus and Clara Reynolds Ellis, build "The Big House." He and his sister, Kathleen Ellis Ryals, moved into the "The Big House" as children. The farmland produced sugar cane, peanuts, and cotton, and was worked by mules.

Ned brought his wife, May Marshall Green, as a bride to "The Big House." There she was taught to cook by an old lady who lived on the farm, Classie Clara Cella Perdue. Classie Clara Cella has done us all a favor by teaching May to cook!

Soups

Wild Rice and Asparagus Soup With Ham

1 (5-oz.) package Mahatma Long Grain Wild Rice With Seasonings
1-1/2 cups water
1 (10-oz.) package frozen asparagus, partially thawed
4 tablespoons margarine
1 large onion, chopped
3 large cloves garlic, minced
1/2 cup plain flour
5 cups chicken broth
1 teaspoon salt
1/2 teaspoon black pepper
1 bay leaf
1/2 teaspoon thyme
2 cups cooked, diced ham
2 cups Half and Half
1-1/2 cups milk
Paprika

In a medium saucepan, bring the water to a boil; then add the wild rice. Cover pan, and reduce heat to simmer. Cook rice about 20 to 25 minutes, until tender. Cut the partially thawed asparagus spears into thin slices. In a Dutch oven, melt the margarine, and saute the onion, garlic, and asparagus slices until tender. Slowly stir in the flour to keep the mixture smooth; then slowly stir in the chicken broth, keeping the mixture smooth. Add salt and pepper; then add bay leaf, thyme, and ham. Simmer for 20 minutes. Remove and discard bay leaf; then stir in the Half and Half and the milk. Heat to serving temperature; do not allow to boil. Stir in the wild rice. Cook and stir, below boiling, for an additional 5 minutes. Serve hot, sprinkled with paprika. Serves 8.

Alice's Matzo Ball Soup

1 tablespoon margarine, melted	4 cups cooked, chopped, salted
2 eggs, beaten	chicken
1/2 cup matzo meal	8 cups chicken broth
3 tablespoons seltzer water	3 large peeled carrots, divided
2 teaspoons salt, divided	2 stalks celery, diced
4 teaspoons finely chopped	1 large onion, diced
fresh parsley, divided	1 bay leaf

In a medium bowl, combine the margarine and eggs; then stir in the matzo meal, seltzer water, 1 teaspoon of the salt, and 1 teaspoon of the parsley. Cover bowl, and refrigerate for about 20 minutes. In a Dutch oven, add the chicken, the broth, 1 of the carrots diced, celery, onion, bay leaf, and the remaining teaspoon salt; bring to a boil. Reduce heat, and simmer for 30 minutes. After matzo mixture has chilled, form into 1/2-inch balls, and refrigerate until very firm. After the 30-minute cooking time of the soup, and the matzo balls are firmly chilled, bring soup to a boil, and drop the matzo balls into the soup. Reduce heat to simmer, and cook until matzo balls are completely done, about 30 minutes. Slice the remaining carrots thin, and add to the soup after 20 minutes of cooking time to cook the remaining 10 minutes. Discard the bay leaf; then add the remaining parsley just before serving. Serve hot.

This is a traditional Jewish soup always served to celebrate the Passover holiday. It is also greatly enjoyed in many non-Jewish homes. Alice Westbrook Roberts, my sister by marriage, remembers her step-grandmother, Florence Harris (or Flossie as she was lovingly known), making this most delicious soup.

Madie's Divine Oyster and Artichoke Soup

2 pints fresh small oysters,
   undrained
2 green onions minced with tops
4 tablespoons margarine or
   butter
5 tablespoons plain flour
1 (14-oz.) can artichoke hearts,
   undrained
2 cups chicken broth
1 teaspoon or cube chicken
   bouillon
1 tablespoon Worcestershire
   sauce

2 whole bay leaves
10 to 12 oz. fresh washed
   spinach leaves (no stems),
   well chopped, or 1 (10-oz.)
   package frozen chopped
   spinach; thawed,
   drained, and pressed dry
1 teaspoon freshly ground black
   pepper
1 teaspoon Cavender's Greek
   Seasoning
Paprika for garnish

Pour the oysters in a strainer over a bowl to catch the oyster liquid; set aside. In a Dutch oven, saute the green onions in the margarine until soft. Gradually stir in the flour, keeping the mixture smooth. Then gradually stir in the liquid from the artichoke hearts, keeping the mixture smooth. Stir in the oyster liquid, chicken broth, and chicken bouillon. Bring the soup to a boil; then reduce heat to simmer, and stir constantly until thickened. Cut the artichoke hearts into quarters, and add to the soup; then stir in the Worcestershire sauce and bay leaves. Add spinach, pepper, and Cavender's Seasoning. Stir and simmer for 30 minutes. After 30 minutes, use a fork to lift the oysters from the strainer avoiding shells, etc., and drop the oysters into the soup. Simmer the soup with the oysters for an additional 30 minutes. Remove bay leaves, and taste the soup. Because of varying saltiness of oysters, it is difficult to give specific seasoning ingredients. After tasting, if the soup is not salty enough, add an additional 1 teaspoon Cavender's Greek Seasoning and/or 1 teaspoon chicken bouillon. Serve hot with lots of paprika to garnish.

Cheesy Potato Soup

All vegetables including the potatoes can be cut in a food processor, if desired. The potatoes will be shredded instead of cubed. This is a quicker method of making the soup.

2 tablespoons margarine, melted
2 stalks celery, sliced
1 medium onion, chopped
1 clove garlic, minced

6 medium Idaho potatoes, peeled and cubed
3 cups water
5 teaspoons granulated chicken bouillon
3/4 teaspoon seasoned salt
2 cups milk
2 cups grated sharp Cheddar cheese
Freshly chopped chives
Paprika

In a Dutch oven, melt margarine, and saute the celery, onion, and garlic until tender. Add potatoes, water, bouillon, and seasoned salt; bring to a boil. Cover and reduce heat to simmer. Cook, stirring often, until all ingredients are very tender. Remove from heat, and mash all the vegetables with a potato masher, leaving the mixture slightly lumpy. Add milk and cheese; then cook over low heat, while stirring, until cheese is melted. Serve hot topped with chives and paprika. Serves 4 to 6.

Christmas Bayou Gumbo

Make one day before serving. Freezes very well.

2 quarts turkey or chicken
  broth
2 large onions, chopped
6 large ribs celery, chopped
1 medium green pepper,
  chopped
4 medium cloves garlic, minced
2 tablespoons dried parsley
  flakes
2 large bay leaves
1 (28-oz.) can tomatoes, chopped
1 (15-oz.) can tomato sauce
2-1/2 teaspoons salt
1 teaspoon black pepper

3 cups diced, cooked turkey or
  chicken
4 tablespoons Worcestershire
  sauce
4 drops liquid crab boil (be
  precise)
2 lbs. or more seafood (optional)
  use shrimp, whole crabs,
  oysters, crawfish in any
  combination, or omit seafood
  altogether. (Do not use fish.)
10-oz. fresh or frozen okra,
  sliced
4 drops Tabasco sauce (optional)
2 tablespoons file
Hot rice

In a large Dutch oven, add broth, onions, celery, green peppers, garlic, parsley, bay leaves, chopped tomatoes, tomato sauce, salt, and pepper; stir. Bring to a boil, and reduce heat to simmer. Cook, uncovered, for 1 hour. Bring gumbo to a boil, and add turkey or chicken, Worcestershire sauce, crab boil, and seafood, if desired; reduce heat, and simmer 1 hour. Add okra, and simmer 1/2 hour. Taste test for additional salt; then add Tabasco, if desired. Place the file in a small bowl, and add some hot gumbo to mix; return file mixture to gumbo pot. Simmer for another 1/2 hour, stirring frequently. Allow gumbo to cool, and refrigerate overnight. When ready to serve, reheat very slowly; stir often, being careful not to let the gumbo stick. Remove bay leaves, and discard. Serve over hot rice in soup bowls. Serves 8-10.

Poling yo pirogue on da bayou keepin' yo eye out fo gator on a chill day atta Christmas, a hot bowl of da gumbo would tase right some good!

Ann's Homemade Chicken and Vegetable Soup

1 chicken fryer, split in half	10 okra pods, sliced
Salt	1 (28-oz.) can tomatoes, mashed
Water	1/2 of a 20-oz. bag frozen
1 teaspoon freshly ground black	vegetable soup mix
pepper	4 oz. vermicelli, uncooked and
2 carrots, sliced	broken in half
3 ribs celery, chopped	Additional salt and pepper
1 large onion, chopped	to taste

Wash fryer halves, and remove all extra fat; then generously salt the halves, and set aside. Fill a Dutch oven 1/2 full of water, and begin bringing water to a boil. While water is heating, prepare the vegetables. When water boils, add chicken halves and pepper to the boiling water. Cover and reduce heat to a low rolling boil. Cook chicken until very tender and beginning to fall off the bone; then remove chicken to a bowl, and cool. Add all vegetables to the chicken broth, and bring to a full boil; reduce heat to simmer, and cook, uncovered. While vegetables are cooking, skin and bone the chicken; then chop the chicken, discarding the skin and bones. Add chopped chicken to the soup while the vegetables are still cooking. Continue to cook until vegetables are tender, plus an additional 20 minutes. Bring soup back to a full boil, and slowly add vermicelli pieces. Reduce heat to simmer for 10 minutes. Taste to adjust salt and pepper. Serve hot.

Low Country Boíl

5 lbs. headless, fresh, medium-size shrimp; unpeeled	2 to 3 lbs. small new or red potatoes, washed and unpeeled
3 quarts water	
1 (6-oz.) can Old Bay Seasoning	2 to 4 lbs. spicy Kielbasa sausage, sliced
5 tablespoons salt	
1 quart white vinegar	12 small partial ears frozen corn-on-the-cob
2 large onions, peeled and quartered	
	Cleaned blue crab backs, as many as desired (optional)

Place shrimp into a large bowl or pot filled with cold water, and stir vigorously with a large spoon for a few seconds. Pour the shrimp into a colander to drain. Repeat this process 5 more times. Do not cheat! Select a large pot that will easily accommodate all of the ingredients. Put the water, the entire contents of the can of Old Bay Seasoning, salt, and vinegar into the pot; bring to a boil. Add onions, small potatoes, and uncooked sausage; boil for 10 minutes. Add corn; boil for 7 minutes. Add washed shrimp and crab backs to boiling mixture, and stir. Allow the shrimp and crab to cook until shrimp turn pink, plus 2 minutes. Sometimes the temperature does not return to a boil before the shrimp are cooked. Do not overcook. Remove pot from the heat, and allow to sit for exactly 5 minutes; then immediately pour off the liquid, and spread contents of pot on large platters to start cooling. It is important to spread the Low Country Boil; if it stays piled up, then it continues to cook and will overcook the shrimp.

Dive in! This is a full meal. The only accompaniments needed are butter; lots of good cocktail sauce (see next page); hot, crusty French bread; bone-yards (bowls or plates to hold shrimp and crab shells); plenty of time; and good company. Often the table is covered with layers of newspapers which can be rolled-up after the feast and discarded. You can throw in a salad or slaw for something green.

cocktail sauce

2 cups catsup	4 drops Tabasco sauce
8 tablespoons pure horseradish (not creamed)	6 tablespoons lemon juice

Mix all ingredients. Sauce may be stored in the refrigerator in a tightly covered jar. Makes 2 cups.

cold winter's Night chicken Soup

1 whole chicken fryer, washed and cleaned	5 teaspoons chicken bouillon
Water	4 Idaho potatoes, peeled and cubed
1/4 cup olive oil	1/2 teaspoon salt
2 cloves garlic, minced	1 teaspoon freshly ground black pepper
1 cup diced carrots	6 oz. wide egg noodles
1 cup diced celery	Additional salt, if desired
1 cup diced onions	Paprika

Put the whole chicken in a Dutch oven, and barely cover with water. Add olive oil and garlic; bring to a high boil. Reduce heat to low boil; cover and cook until chicken is very tender and falling off the bones. Remove chicken to a bowl to drain and cool. Add carrots, celery, onions, bouillon, potatoes, salt, and pepper to the chicken broth. Bring soup to a high boil; then reduce to a low boil, cover, and cook until potatoes are almost tender. While soup is cooking, remove and discard the bones from the chicken. Chop the chicken, and add to the soup while potatoes are cooking. When potatoes are almost tender, add the noodles; cover and simmer for 10 minutes. When the noodles are done, taste the soup for salt, and add, if desired. Serve soup hot, sprinkled with paprika.

Salads

vinaigrette shrimp salad

Make 3 to 4 hours in advance.

2 lbs. fresh, medium-size shrimp, cooked in salted water and peeled
8 oz. small white mushrooms, thinly sliced
1 small sweet red pepper, cut in thin strips
1 (10-oz.) package frozen snow peas, thawed
1 cup pecans, toasted and chopped
Pretty lettuce
Fresh tomato wedges

Sauce:

1 tablespoon Dijon-style mustard
1 clove garlic, minced
1/2 teaspoon lemon juice
4 tablespoons cider vinegar
1 cup vegetable oil
1/2 teaspoon salt
1/4 teaspoon freshly ground black pepper

In a large bowl, combine the whole shrimp, mushrooms, peppers, snow peas, and pecans. To make the sauce, use a food processor or blender, mix the mustard, garlic, lemon juice, and vinegar; blend. Then, running the machine continuously, add the oil in a slow, steady stream. Add salt and pepper. Pour the sauce on the shrimp mixture, and toss to mix completely. Taste and add salt, if desired. Cover bowl, and refrigerate for 2 to 3 hours. Serve cold on pretty lettuce with a tomato wedge for topping.

Chinese Chicken Salad in Baskets

Baskets:	Vegetable shortening 12 egg roll skins

Use a 1-quart, glass, microwave-safe bowl. Invert bowl, and lightly grease bottom with vegetable shortening. Place 1 egg roll skin over the bowl, and press to form shape of bowl. Microwave on high for 1 minute. Check the basket; it should be crisp and light colored. If it is not, microwave another 15 seconds. Watch carefully; they burn easily. Remove basket from bowl to a wire rack to cool. Repeat with all egg roll skins.

Sauce:	
1/4 cup vegetable oil	4 tablespoons soy sauce
2 teaspoons sesame oil	4 tablespoons rice wine vinegar
1 teaspoon granulated sugar	1/2 teaspoon ground ginger

In a small bowl, mix both oils, sugar, soy sauce, vinegar, and ginger. Beat vigorously with a fork until well blended.

Salad:	1 (8-oz.) can sliced water chestnuts, drained
1 lb. cooked chicken, cut in thin strips	1/2 to 1 (10-oz.) package frozen snow peas, thawed
1/2 bunch radishes, thinly sliced	1 small head iceberg or specialty lettuce, finely shredded
6 green onions, thinly sliced with tops	Paprika

In a large bowl, mix all salad ingredients except lettuce and paprika, with half of the sauce. Pour a small amount of sauce on the shredded lettuce, and toss to coat. Put remaining sauce in a small pitcher. At serving time (no earlier), fill baskets with lettuce; then top with chicken salad. Sprinkle with paprika or other garnish. Serve remaining sauce on the side.

Be sure to break and eat the baskets as part of the meal.

chicken Salad Supreme

1/2 cup sour cream	3/4 cup toasted pecans, chopped
1/2 cup mayonnaise	(reserve 1/4 cup to garnish)
1-1/2 teaspoons salt	4 slices bacon, cooked
1 tablespoon lemon juice	and crumbled
1 tablespoon soy sauce	1 cup sliced green onions
2 cups diced celery	1/2 teaspoon paprika
4 oz. mushrooms, chopped	4 cups cooked, chopped chicken

In a large bowl, mix all ingredients, except chicken and reserved pecans, and blend. Add chicken, and mix completely. Cover and refrigerate for several hours before serving. Top with the reserved pecans. Serves 6.

Feta Spinach Salad with Pecans

1 bunch tender fresh spinach	1/2 medium red onion, sliced
1 small avocado, peeled and	thin in rings
thinly sliced	4 oz. crumbled feta cheese
	1/2 cup coarsely chopped pecans

Dressing:	
1/2 cup olive oil	1/2 teaspoon freshly ground
1/4 cup red wine vinegar	black pepper
1 tablespoon dried basil,	1 teaspoon granulated sugar
crumbled	1 large clove garlic, minced
1/2 teaspoon salt	and crushed

Wash spinach very carefully, and remove large stems; drain until completely dry. Tear spinach into bite-size pieces, and put into a large bowl. Make the dressing by blending all of the dressing ingredients in a food processor or blender. Add all remaining ingredients to the spinach, and pour on the desired amount of dressing. Toss several times to mix well before serving.

Far East Chicken Salad

Make several hours in advance.

2 tablespoons margarine
1 (2.38-oz.) jar or 8 tablespoons
   sesame seeds
2-1/2 oz. sliced almonds

2 packages Ramen Chicken
  Flavored Noodles, slightly
  crumbled
2 cups cooked, chopped chicken
3 cups finely shredded green
   cabbage
1 bunch green onions, chopped
   with tops

Dressing:

6 tablespoons rice vinegar
1 tablespoon granulated sugar
1 teaspoon salt

1 tablespoon freshly ground
   black pepper
   (yes, tablespoon)
1 cup vegetable oil
Flavor envelopes from the
  Ramen Noodles

In a skillet, melt the margarine, and lightly brown the sesame seeds, almonds, and dry noodles. In a large bowl, combine the sesame seed mixture with the remaining salad ingredients, and toss to mix. In another bowl, mix all dressing ingredients, and beat well to blend. Pour the dressing over the salad mixture, and toss to mix completely. Cover and refrigerate for several hours before serving cold. Serves 4 to 6.

Italian Green Pea Salad

Make 3 to 4 hours in advance.

1 (10-oz.) package frozen small
green peas, thawed
1 cup thinly sliced celery
1 small sweet red pepper, cut in
thin short strips

1/2 small green pepper, cut in
thin short strips
3 green onions, thinly sliced
with tops
1/2 cup prepared Italian
salad dressing
1/4 teaspoon salt

In a large bowl, combine all of the vegetables, and mix. Pour on the salad dressing; then sprinkle with the salt, and toss to mix. Cover bowl, and refrigerate for 2 to 3 hours. Serve cold on lettuce leaf cups or in a lettuce-lined bowl.

Roman Potato Salad

Make several hours or 1 day in advance.

3 lbs. Idaho potatoes
2 medium fresh tomatoes, cut in
thin wedges

1/2 medium green pepper,
finely diced
1 large onion, finely diced

Sauce:

1/2 cup olive oil
1/2 cup red wine vinegar
2 cloves garlic, minced
2 tablespoons Parmesan cheese

1 tablespoon chopped parsley
1-3/4 teaspoons salt
1 teaspoon coarsely ground
black pepper
1/2 teaspoon liquid red hot
sauce (do not use Tabasco)

Bake or boil unpeeled potatoes until tender (do not use salt.) Allow potatoes to completely cool. While potatoes are cooling, mix together all of the sauce ingredients; set aside. When potatoes are cool, peel and dice. Place potatoes in a large bowl, and add tomato wedges, green pepper, and onion. Pour the sauce on the salad, and gently toss to mix. Cover bowl, and refrigerate for several hours or overnight before serving. Serve cold.

May's Angel Salad

The color of the salad is very light, which lends itself to most any color combination used for a theme. Use red and green cherries, fresh mint sprigs, etc. The salad may be made in individual molds, ramekins, a shallow glass dish, or a pretty bowl.

2 envelopes plain gelatin	1 cup crushed pineapple,
3/4 cup cool tap water	drained
1 cup granulated sugar	1 cup pecans, chopped
1-1/2 cups boiling water	1/2 pint cream, whipped, or 1
1 cup Hellmann's mayonnaise	cup whipped topping

In a large bowl, empty the contents of both gelatin envelopes in the bowl, and pour the COOL water over the gelatin. Allow to stand until it is completely softened; then stir in the sugar. Measure the boiling water into the cup after the water is boiling. Add the boiling water to the gelatin mixture, and immediately stir vigorously to dissolve the gelatin and sugar completely. Refrigerate this mixture, and watch carefully until it thickens; remove from the refrigerator before it congeals or it will never make properly. After removing from the refrigerator, stir in the mayonnaise, drained pineapple, and chopped pecans. Fold in the whipped cream, and pour into the container of choice. Cover and refrigerate until very firmly set.

This is a long-time favorite of the Green family. May Marshall Green Ellis makes this recipe to perfection. It is also delicious as a dessert.

Ellen's
Strawberry Pretzel Salad

This can be made in a 9- x 13-inch size or 8- x 8-inch size. Depending on salad thickness desired. It is a 3-layer salad.

2 cups crushed salted pretzels
3/4 cup melted margarine

1 cup plus 3 tablespoons granulated sugar, divided
8 oz. cream cheese, softened
8 oz. whipped topping
2 cups boiling water
1 (6-oz.) package strawberry Jello
1 (10-oz.) package frozen sliced strawberries, thawed

Preheat oven to 350 degrees. In a medium bowl, mix crushed pretzels, margarine, and 3 tablespoons of the sugar. Press this mixture into the bottom of an attractive, shallow 9- x 13-inch baking dish. Bake in the preheated oven for 5 to 8 minutes; do not overbake. Allow crust to cool. In a electric mixer, cream the remaining sugar with the cream cheese; then add the whipped topping until blended. Spread the cream cheese mixture over the cooled crust, and set aside. In a large bowl, add the boiling water to the Jello, and stir vigorously to COMPLETELY dissolve. Add thawed strawberries, and mix. Refrigerate this mixture until it begins to thicken; do not let it set. Pour the thickened strawberry mixture over the cream cheese layer; cover and return to the refrigerator to completely set. Cut into squares to serve.

Ellen Ellis Burkett makes this absolutely wonderful salad. It has beautiful color and great crunchy texture to enhance the congealed salad layer.

Sour Cream Potato Salad

Make several hours in advance or the day before serving.
8 medium Idaho potatoes
1-1/2 cups sour cream
1-1/2 cups mayonnaise
1/2 cup Durkee's Famous Dressing

1 medium onion, chopped fine
2 tablespoons parsley or
   parsley flakes
1 teaspoon salt
1 teaspoon celery seed
1 teaspoon horseradish

Bake or boil unpeeled potatoes until tender. Cool to handle; then peel and set aside. In a medium bowl, mix all remaining ingredients. When potatoes have cooled, slice thin. In a shallow 2-quart casserole dish, make thin layers beginning with potato slices; then spread sour cream mixture. Repeat layers until all potatoes are used. Final layer should be sour cream mixture. Garnish top with available herbs, spices, or colorful vegetables. Cover bowl, and refrigerate for several hours or overnight.

Auburn Sandwich

1 fresh, ripe tomato
1 mild onion
Dill or bread-and-butter pickles
8 slices of white bread
Mayonnaise

4 potatoes
Vegetable oil
Salt to taste
8 strips bacon, cooked crisp

Slice in thin rounds the tomato, onion, and pickles; set aside. Toast bread, and spread with mayonnaise; set aside. Peel and slice potatoes thin; then fry in vegetable oil until potatoes are tender, brown, and crisp. Drain on paper towel. Salt potatoes and tomatoes to taste. Assemble sandwich by placing all ingredients including bacon on the toast; cut in half, and enjoy.

Thomas Ellis remembers this sandwich being a part of his Auburn University college days. A customer of his wife, Melissa, would bring the sandwiches to her at the bank, where she worked. The sandwiches were named for the customer, who had a rather unusual nickname that didn't bring food to mind! The next time you see Thomas ask him the original name!

Ann's Asparagus and Pecan Salad

Make ahead of time. It may be made as long as 36 hours in advance.

1-1/2 lbs. fresh asparagus (use only young and tender) or 2 (10-oz.) packages frozen asparagus spears

2 tablespoons vegetable oil
1/4 cup cider vinegar
1/4 cup soy sauce
1 tablespoon granulated sugar
3/4 cup pecans, finely chopped
1/4 teaspoon ground black pepper

Cook asparagus in boiling, salted, water about 6 to 7 minutes or until just tender. Do not overcook. Drain; then rinse under cold water, and drain again. Place the drained asparagus in a shallow baking dish in a single layer. In a bowl, mix the remaining ingredients, and pour over the asparagus. Tilt the baking dish several times to allow the marinade to flow over the asparagus spears. Cover and refrigerate. Tilt baking dish several more times before serving to marinate evenly. Serves 6 to 8.

A rather unusual choice of ingredients that come together for a special taste treat.

Mandarin Almond Salad

1/4 cup sliced almonds
1 tablespoon plus 1 teaspoon
  granulated sugar
1/3 head each of 2 different
  specialty lettuces; ie. bibb,
  romaine, red tip, iceberg, etc.

1 (11-oz.) can mandarin oranges
1 cup thinly sliced celery
2 green onions, thinly sliced with
  tops

Dressing:

1/4 cup vegetable oil
2 tablespoons white vinegar
2 tablespoons granulated sugar

1 tablespoon chopped fresh
  parsley
1/2 teaspoon salt
Dash of black pepper
Dash of Tabasco sauce

Saute almonds and sugar in a small heavy skillet for about 20 minutes until almonds are caramelized; set aside. Break the 2 kinds of lettuce into bite-size pieces in a large bowl. Add drained mandarin oranges, celery, and green onions; mix. Cover bowl, and refrigerate. Make the dressing by combining all dressing ingredients in a glass jar with a tight-fitting lid. Shake vigorously to blend and dissolve all ingredients; refrigerate. About 30 minutes before serving time, remove salad dressing from refrigerator. Allow dressing to come to room temperature for 20 minutes. Pour salad dressing over the salad, and toss well to mix. Just before serving sprinkle the almonds on top of the salad.

Rave Reviews Slaw

There's a secret to this slaw recipe--how the cabbage is shredded! Select a hard, non-leafy cabbage, and cut into quarters. To get long, thin shreds of cabbage, finely shred the quartered cabbage on the longest surface with a steel-blade vegetable slicer, or use a sharp knife and shred by hand. The slaw does not taste the same if it is chopped or coarse. Of course, it takes longer to do this; but it is worth the effort for the taste.

4 cups thinly shredded cabbage, packed firmly in the cup	1 teaspoon salt
1 large, fresh, ripe tomato, diced	2 tablespoons vegetable oil
1/2 large green pepper, diced	2 tablespoons white vinegar
	Additional salt to taste

Place the shredded cabbage in a large bowl with room to toss. Add diced tomatoes and green pepper; then toss to mix. Sprinkle the salt evenly over the slaw; then drizzle on the oil. Toss the slaw a good number of times to completely coat the vegetables; then sprinkle with the vinegar. Toss several more times to blend in the vinegar. Taste for salt, and add, if needed. Serve immediately, or cover and refrigerate until serving time.

This is a very low-calorie, low-fat, fresh vegetable dish with outstanding flavor. It lasts several days in the refrigerator and is perfect as a side dish or on corned beef, ham, or pastrami sandwiches. You will definitely get rave reviews when you serve it. Bow and smile as you receive your applause!

cajun Slaw

Your cabbage will be best shredded in long, thin, fine pieces for this slaw.

2 cups shredded green cabbage
2 cups shredded red cabbage
1 small onion
1 carrot, grated (optional)
1/4 cup chopped green pepper
   (optional)
1/3 cup white vinegar

1/4 cup vegetable oil
1/2 teaspoon sugar
1 teaspoon salt
1/2 teaspoon dry mustard
1/2 teaspoon celery salt
1/4 teaspoon Tabasco sauce

Shred the cabbages, and pack into cup to measure. Slice the onion as thin as possible; then chop. Add the carrot and green pepper, if desired. In a glass bowl, combine onion, vinegar, oil, sugar, salt, dry mustard, celery salt, Tabasco sauce. Mix well; then pour over the shredded vegetables. Toss until very well blended; cover and refrigerate until serving time. Serves 6.

Summertime Salad

Make 3 to 4 hours in advance.

1 (16-oz.) package frozen petite
   lima beans
1 tablespoon margarine
1 (16-oz.) package frozen white
   shoe peg corn
1/4 cup diced green pepper
1/4 cup diced sweet red pepper

1-1/2 teaspoons dried onion
   flakes
1/4 to 1/3 cup mayonnaise
1/4 cup cooked, crumbled bacon
   (optional)
1/4 teaspoon freshly ground
   black pepper
Salt to taste

Cook lima beans by package directions with salt until tender; do not overcook. In a skillet, melt margarine, and quickly stir-fry corn until tender-crisp. In a large bowl, mix cooked and drained lima beans and cooked corn; then add all remaining ingredients. Mix well, and taste for salt. Additional mayonnaise and bacon may be added, if desired. Cover and refrigerate for 2 hours. Serve cold.

Royal Rice Salad

Make salad 3 to 4 hours in advance.

1 package chicken flavor,
   Rice-A-Roni
1 cup cubed, cooked ham
1/4 teaspoon curry powder
   (optional)

1 cup black olives, chopped
1 jar marinated artichoke
   hearts, drained and chopped
1/2 cup chopped onion
1/2 cup chopped green pepper
1/2 cup slivered almonds

Additions: Lettuce, tomato slices, or scooped-out tomato cups, if desired.

Cook rice according to package directions, and cool. In a large bowl, mix the cooled rice with all the remaining ingredients except the additions. Cover and refrigerate for 2 to 3 hours. Serve on lettuce topped with tomato slices or on lettuce topped with a tomato cup filled with the salad.

Caesar Salad Dressing

3 cups mayonnaise
1 (2-oz.) tin anchovies, drained
1/2 cup lemon juice
1/4 cup Parmesan cheese

2 tablespoons Worcestershire
   sauce
1/4 teaspoon freshly ground
   black pepper

In a small food processor or blender, mix and blend all ingredients into a salad dressing. Refrigerate dressing in a jar with a tight-fitting lid for several hours before using. Keep refrigerated.

Honey Dijon Mustard Dressing

1 tablespoon Dijon-style mustard	1/3 cup minced onion
2 tablespoons honey	1 teaspoon fresh minced parsley
2/3 cup mayonnaise	Juice of 1/2 small lemon
1/4 cup vegetable oil	

Combine all ingredients in a small food processor or blender until smooth and blended. Refrigerate in a glass jar with a tight-fitting lid to store.

Poppy Seed Salad Dressing

Perfect salad dressing for a mixed green salad or for fruit salad. If double the recipe is desired, double all ingredients except the poppy seeds.

2/3 cup vegetable oil	5 teaspoons minced onion
1/3 cup honey	4 teaspoons Dijon-style mustard
1/4 cup red wine vinegar	1 teaspoon salt
5 teaspoons poppy seeds	

Combine all ingredients in a food processor or blender, and blend into a salad dressing. Pour into a glass jar with a tight-fitting lid, and refrigerate for several hours before serving. Shake well before using. Keep refrigerated to store.

Stories from the
victorian verandah

The upstairs Ghost

Before May Green had married into the Ellis Family, owners of Priester's Pecan Company, a great-aunt had lived upstairs in "The Big House." She was quite an eccentric, never venturing downstairs. It was her custom to "air-out" everything, particularly food and clothing. In her mind, this was to prevent any possible poisonings. One of her pastimes was spitting out of the upstairs windows, to the constant horror of those below!

After May became a member of the family, she had been told of Aunt Ginny's antics, and that her ghost lived upstairs. One very cold winter night, when her husband, Ned, was away, May and her household help, Christine, were alone in "The Big House" for the night. They had strung up a heavy curtain across the main stairway to keep the heat downstairs. Suddenly, May and Christine heard a noise on the stairwell behind the curtain. Christine flung open the door and went screaming out into the yard, declaring "Oh, Lawd, Aunt Ginny's comin' down the stairs, and she's gonna git us!" When May persuaded Christine to return to the house, Aunt Ginny was nowhere in sight, but there seemed to be several pecan pralines missing from the silver bowl on the sideboard . . .

Beef

Madaris'
Argentine Style
Grilled Tenderloin

1 (3-lb.) beef tenderloin, trimmed of fat	1 tablespoon freshly ground coarse black pepper
1/2 cup olive oil	2 tablespoons red wine vinegar
3 large garlic cloves, minced	Salt and pepper to taste after grilling
2 tablespoons fresh minced parsley	

Slice the tenderloin into 3/4- to 1-inch-thick pieces. In a large glass bowl, combine the olive oil, garlic, parsley, pepper, and vinegar; mix to blend. Add the tenderloin slices; cover and refrigerate for 1-1/2 hours. After the marinade time, remove the bowl from the refrigerator, and turn the tenderloin slices. Allow the slices to come to room temperature in the marinade; then discard the marinade. Grill on high as soon as the tenderloin is room temperature. Cook 2 to 2-1/2 minutes per side or to desired doneness. Salt and pepper to taste immediately after removing from the grill. Serves 6 to 8.

This beef will absolutely melt in your mouth. It's a masterpiece of flavor and texture. A definite must for cattle ranchers such as Katie Ellis and Chuck Madaris III, and their children Kathleen and Charlie.

Grilled Flank Steak

Marinate 4 to 6 hours.

	1/2 teaspoon chopped garlic
1 flank steak	2 tablespoons olive oil
2 tablespoons soy sauce	2 tablespoons catsup
1 teaspoon ground ginger	Salt and pepper to taste

Place flank steak in a glass baking dish just large enough for steak to fit flat. Combine all marinade ingredients except salt and pepper in a bowl, and blend well. Pour marinade over steak; cover and refrigerate for 4 to 6 hours. Turn the steak several times to marinate evenly. About 1/2 hour before cooking time, remove the steak from the refrigerator, and discard marinade. Cook on medium-hot grill for about 6 minutes per side. Immediately after removing from grill, salt and pepper both sides to taste. Slice thin to serve.

Grilled Marinated Sirloin

4 teaspoons lemon juice	1 large 1-to 1-1/2-inch-thick
1/2 cup Worcestershire sauce	sirloin steak
1/2 cup cola soda	Salt
1 cup dry white wine	Coarsely ground black pepper

In a shallow glass 2-quart baking dish, mix all liquid ingredients; then add the steak. Allow steak to marinate for several hours in the refrigerator. Turn several times to marinate evenly. Remove the steak from the refrigerator 1/2 hour before cooking time. Cook on a medium grill for 3 minutes per side; turn once, using tongs to avoid loosing juices by piercing the steak with a fork. To test for desired doneness, make a small slit in the center of the steak. Immediately after removing steak from grill, salt and pepper to taste.

Sirloin and Snow Peas

8 oz. sirloin beefsteak	6 oz. frozen snow peas or sugar
2 tablespoons cornstarch,	snaps, thawed
divided	2 tablespoons peanut oil or
3 tablespoons soy sauce, divided	vegetable oil, divided
1 tablespoon cooking sherry	1 large onion, sliced in rings
1 large clove garlic, minced	Salt and pepper to taste
1/4 teaspoon crushed red	1 medium fresh tomato, diced
pepper flakes	Hot white rice
3/4 cup water	

Slice the steak into thin strips. In a medium bowl, combine 1 tablespoon of the cornstarch with 1 tablespoon of the soy sauce, sherry, and garlic. Add steak slices, and allow to marinate for 15 minutes. In a small bowl, combine remaining cornstarch and soy with the crushed red pepper flakes and water. Stir to blend, and set aside. Remove tips and any strings from the snow peas. Drain marinade from the steak, and discard. In a large skillet, heat 1 tablespoon of the oil to very hot, but not smoking. Add steak, and stir-fry for 1 minute; then remove beef to a side plate. Add the remaining oil to the skillet, and heat. Stir-fry the snow peas or sugar snaps and onion rings until tender-crisp. Salt and pepper to taste. Return the steak to the skillet along with the reserved cornstarch mixture and the diced tomato. Cook until thickened, heated, and the tomato is softened. Serve over hot white rice. Serves 4.

Australian Beef Puff Pie

1-1/2 lbs. tender beef, minced	Pinch of nutmeg
2 teaspoons granulated beef bouillon or cubes	3 tablespoons plain flour
3 cups water, divided	1 teaspoon soy sauce
1/2 teaspoon salt	1/4 teaspoon Tabasco sauce
1/2 teaspoon fresh, coarsely ground black pepper	Folded commercial refrigerator pie crust, unbaked

Pie Top:

1 sheet of a (17-oz.) package frozen puff pastry, thawed	1 egg yolk
	1 teaspoon water

Beef Filling: In a large skillet, brown the minced beef. Add bouillon, two cups of the water, salt, pepper, and nutmeg to the beef. Bring beef mixture to boiling; cover and reduce heat to simmer for 20 minutes. Remove skillet from heat. In a small bowl, stir the remaining water into the flour until smooth. Add flour mixture to the beef, and return to heat. Stir and heat until meat mixture thickens; then stir in the soy sauce, and Tabasco sauce. Simmer, uncovered, for an additional 5 to 10 minutes; then remove from heat, and allow to become cold. When filling is cold, spread in the bottom of the unbaked pie crust. Preheat oven and a baking sheet to 450 degrees.

Pie Top: Lightly flour a board, and roll out the puff pastry. Cut a round to completely cover the top of the pie. Wet edges of the pie with extra water, and gently press puff pastry top into place. Trim around edges with a sharp knife. Pierce center of pie several times with a pointed knife. In a small bowl, beat the egg yolk and water to mix; then brush top of pie with the egg yolk mixture. Bake in the preheated oven for 5 to 10 minutes or until golden brown; reduce heat to 350 degrees, and cook an additional 10 minutes.

Grilled Chuck Eye Steaks

1/4 cup A-1 Steak Sauce	1/4 teaspoon Tabasco sauce
2 tablespoons packed brown	4 boneless beef chuck eye steaks,
sugar	1-inch thick
2 tablespoons lemon juice	Salt to taste

In a large bowl, mix A-1 Steak Sauce, brown sugar, lemon juice, and Tabasco sauce. Reserve 2 tablespoons of marinade in a small bowl. Place steaks in marinade, and turn to coat all of steak. Allow to marinate for 15 minutes, turning 2 more times. Drain off marinade, and discard. Grill over medium heat for about 5 minutes per side or to desired doneness. Brush with reserved marinade during the last 2 minutes of cooking. Season with salt immediately after removing from grill, if desired. Serves 2 to 3.

Herbed Chuck Beefsteak

Marinate 6 to 24 hours	1 tablespoon Dijon-style
1 lb. boneless beef chuck	mustard
shoulder steak, cut 1-inch	1 tablespoon olive oil
thick	1 clove garlic, minced
1/4 cup minced onion	1/4 teaspoon dried thyme leaves
2 tablespoons chopped parsley	1/4 teaspoon dried basil leaves
2 tablespoons white vinegar	Salt and pepper to taste

Place steak in a Ziplock bag; place steak and bag in a baking pan. In a small bowl, combine remaining ingredients except salt and pepper, and stir until well blended. Pour marinade over steak in bag. Distribute herbs as evenly as possible. Close bag tightly, and marinate in refrigerator for 6 to 24 hours. Turn once or twice to marinate evenly. About 30 minutes before cooking time, remove steak from refrigerator; discard marinade, and allow steak to come to room temperature. Cook on a medium-hot grill for 5 minutes per side. Immediately salt and pepper on both sides after removing from grill. The steak can also be cooked on a broiler pan. Place oven rack to allow steak to be 4 inches from heat. Broil to desired doneness, turning once. Immediately salt and pepper after removing from broiler. Serves 4.

Joe Godbold's Favorite Country Fried Steak

1-1/2 to 2 lbs. round steak	1 small onion
Salt and pepper to taste	1-1/2 to 2 cups water
Plain flour	Hot white rice
3 tablespoons vegetable oil	

Beat the round steak with a mallet. Cut the steak into 1- x 2-inch pieces; then salt and pepper the pieces on all sides. Place flour in a clean plastic bag along with beef, and coat heavily with flour. In a large iron skillet, heat the oil, and pan fry the beef pieces on all sides. Remove fried beef to a side plate. Pour off and discard all but 1 tablespoon of the oil, or add extra oil, if needed to make the 1 tablespoon of oil. In the hot skillet, add 1 tablespoon of flour to the 1 tablespoon hot oil, and brown to make the gravy. Add onion, water, and beef to skillet; then simmer, uncovered, for 1 hour. The gravy can be slightly thinned with water, if desired. Serve over hot white rice.

Lazy Acres Barbecue Beef Brisket

1 to 2 tablespoons margarine	1 (28-oz.) bottle Wicker's
5 to 8 lbs. beef brisket,	Barbecue Marinade
trimmed of fat	and Baste
1/4 cup brown sugar	1 large onion, chopped
	1 (48-oz.) bottle catsup

In a large Dutch oven, melt the margarine, and brown the brisket on both sides. Add all of the remaining ingredients and stir to mix. Bring sauce to a boil; cover and reduce heat to a low simmer. Simmer for 3 hours. Remove brisket after cooking, and cut meat across the grain, or shred. Serve the brisket on warmed hamburger buns with the sauce for sandwiches or as the meat course for dinner. Serves a small herd!

Belgian Beef

3 lbs. boneless beef round roast	2 whole bay leaves
3 tablespoons vegetable oil	1 teaspoon thyme
2 cups sliced onions	1 teaspoon salt
1 clove garlic, minced	1/8 teaspoon coarsely ground
6 oz. V-8 juice	black pepper
1 (12-oz.) can beer	

Trim beef of fat, and cut in cubes. In a Dutch oven, heat oil, and brown beef in batches; remove beef to a side dish. Use remaining juices and oil to saute onions and garlic until tender. Add beef to onion mixture along with remaining ingredients. Bring to a boil; reduce heat to a simmer, and cover. Cook 1 hour or until meat is tender. Remove beef from gravy to a side dish, cover; and keep warm. Continue simmering gravy, uncovered, until reduced to 2 cups of liquid. Spoon gravy over warm beef. Serves 9 to 10.

Leave it to the Belgians to add beer to a recipe. That small country produces at least 400 different brews. The beer adds extra European flavor interest to the beef.

Korean Bulgogi

1 lb. sirloin, partially frozen	2 green onions, sliced with tops
2 tablespoons soy sauce	Dash of ground ginger
1 small clove garlic, minced	2 teaspoons sesame seed
1 teaspoon granulated sugar	1 teaspoon sesame, or vegetable
1/4 teaspoon coarsely ground	oil
black pepper	Hot white rice

Slice beef in thin slices, and place in a glass bowl. In a small bowl, mix soy, garlic, sugar, pepper, green onions, and ginger. Pour sauce over beef; cover and refrigerate for 1 hour. In a skillet, lightly brown sesame seeds in oil; crush seeds, and remove from skillet to a bowl. Heat skillet on high temperature, but not smoking. Quickly stir-fry beef and sauce. Stir in sesame seeds. Serve over hot rice. Serves 3 to 4.

French Beef
With Mushrooms

1 lb. boneless beef sirloin	16 large fresh mushrooms,
1 to 2 tablespoons margarine	cleaned and quartered
Salt to taste	1 medium onion, chopped
1 teaspoon coarsely ground	3 tablespoons plain flour
black pepper	1-1/2 cups beef bouillon
	Hot noodles or rice

Trim the sirloin of all fat; then cut into cubes. In a Dutch oven, brown the cubes of beef on all sides in the margarine. Salt the beef to taste; then add the pepper. Add the mushroom quarters and onions; saute until onions are tender. Sprinkle the beef mixture with flour, and toss gently to coat. Slowly add the bouillon; then cook until thickened. Serve hot over noodles or rice. Serves 3 to 4.

Spicy Pot Roast

3 lbs. beef chuck roast	2 teaspoons crab boil spices
2 tablespoons vegetable oil	1 teaspoon salt
1 cup chopped onion	1 clove garlic, minced
1 cup sliced celery	5 carrots, sliced
1 cup water	5 very small new or red
1/2 cup catsup	potatoes, peeled

In a Dutch oven, brown the roast in hot oil. Add onion, celery, water, catsup, crab boil spices tied in a cloth bag or in a tea ball, salt, and garlic. Cover and simmer for 1 hour. Add more water, if needed. Add sliced carrots and potatoes cut into quarters. Cover and cook an additional 30 minutes or until potatoes are tender. Remove and discard crab boil spices before serving. Serves 6 to 8.

Fantastic Fajitas

Marinate overnight.

1/4 cup soy sauce
4 tablespoons Worcestershire
   sauce
1/4 teaspoon ground cumin
1/2 teaspoon garlic powder
2 lbs. sirloin steak, sliced in
   long strips
1 large green pepper, cut in
   thin strips

1 large sweet red pepper, cut in
   thin strips
1 large mild onion, sliced
   in rings
Medium-size flour tortillas
   wrapped in aluminum foil
   for warming
Salt and pepper to taste,
   after cooking

Additional fillings of choice:

Grated sharp Cheddar cheese
Grated Monterey Jack cheese
Sour cream
Hot refried beans

Chopped tomatoes
Guacamole
Salsa
Etc . . .

In a large glass or plastic bowl, mix together the soy sauce, Worcestershire sauce, cumin, and garlic powder. Add all remaining ingredients, except tortillas, salt, and pepper, and toss well to mix. Cover the bowl, and refrigerate overnight. Stir once or twice while marinating. About 30 minutes before serving, place the foil-wrapped tortillas into a low-heat oven to warm. Then assemble the fillings of choice into serving bowls. When ready to cook fajitas, place the meat and vegetable mixture into a colander to drain. Heat an iron, or other heavy skillet that has been sprayed with spray-oil until very hot, but not smoking. Drop a slice of beef in the hot skillet to test. Beef should sizzle. Add all of the mixture to the hot skillet, and stir-fry until beef is done and vegetables are tender-crisp. Salt and pepper to taste. Place the fajitas on a warm platter to serve. To assemble: Fill a warm tortilla with a small amount of beef mixture; then add any or all of the filling choices, and roll.

This is serious finger food, so eat as best you can! There WILL be fallout, and a fork will come in handy.

Greg's Favorite Oriental Beef

Marinate for 2 to 3 hours in advance.	2 teaspoons cornstarch
	2 medium green peppers, cut in strips
12 oz. sirloin tip or London broil	2 green onions, sliced with tops
2 tablespoons soy sauce	2 teaspoons grated fresh ginger or 1 teaspoon ground ginger
1/2 tablespoon wine vinegar	Hot white rice
1/2 teaspoon granulated sugar	
2 tablespoons vegetable oil, divided	

Trim all fat from beef; then slice thin into Oriental strips. In a medium bowl, combine soy sauce, wine vinegar, sugar, 1 tablespoon of the oil, and the cornstarch; mix to blend. Add beef strips to the bowl, and stir to coat beef. Cover and refrigerate for 2 to 3 hours. When ready to cook, heat 1 tablespoon of the oil in a large skillet until hot but not smoking. Stir-fry the beef until cooked; then remove the beef with a slotted spoon to a side plate. Add the green pepper strips, green onions, and ginger to the hot skillet with a couple of drops of oil, if needed. Stir-fry until green peppers are tender-crisp. Add beef to the vegetables, and stir-fry to heat and blend. Serve immediately over hot white rice. Serves 2 to 4.

Greg Carden, my nephew, is quite a fan of this stir-fry. It really is a meal in itself and so easy to make.

Grilled Chuck Roast

Marinate overnight.

1 (3-lb.) chuck roast
1/3 cup water
1/3 cup brown sugar
1/3 cup soy sauce
1/3 cup bourbon (optional)

1 tablespoon Worcestershire
   sauce
1 teaspoon lemon juice
1/8 teaspoon garlic powder
Salt and pepper to taste
   after grilling

Place roast in a clean plastic bag; then place roast and bag in a baking pan. In a bowl, mix all remaining ingredients until well blended. Pour the marinade over the roast in the bag. Tightly close the bag, and refrigerate overnight. Turn roast several times to marinate evenly. About 1/2 hour before cooking time, remove the roast from the refrigerator, and discard marinade. Sear both sides of the roast on high heat to seal; then grill over low heat for 30 minutes per side. Salt and pepper all over as soon as the roast is removed from the grill. The roast tastes best when served in chunks rather than sliced. Serves 4 to 6.

Savory Crock Pot Roast

Salt and coarsely ground
   black pepper
3 to 4 lb. beef pot roast
1 medium onion, chopped
1 (3/4-oz.) package brown
   gravy mix

1 cup water
1/4 cup chili sauce or catsup
2 teaspoons Dijon-style mustard
1 teaspoon Worcestershire sauce
1/8 teaspoon garlic powder

Salt and pepper the roast on all sides, and place in a crockpot slow cooker. In a medium bowl, combine all of the remaining ingredients until blended, and pour over the roast. Cover and cook on high for 5 hours, or on low for 7 to 8 hours. Remove the roast to slice. If desired, the gravy can be thickened by dissolving a small amount of flour in a small amount of water until smooth. Add the flour mixture to the gravy, and turn crockpot to high. Stir and heat until gravy thickens. Serves 8.

Tijuana Train Wreck Nachos

2 lbs. lean ground chuck or round beef	2 teaspoons crushed oregano
1 large onion, chopped	2 teaspoons salt
2 teaspoons chili powder	2 cloves garlic, minced
2 teaspoons ground cumin	1 (15-oz.) can tomato sauce
	Tortilla chips

Toppings:

	Grated Monterey Jack cheese
	Grated Cheddar cheese
Black olive slices	Jalapeno pepper slices
Chopped tomatoes	Salsa
Chopped onions	Melted Velveeta with salsa
Shredded lettuce	

In a large skillet, cook the ground beef and onions until beef is done; drain. Add the chili powder, cumin, oregano, salt, and minced garlic; cook and stir 1 minute. Stir in the tomato sauce and bring to a boil. Reduce heat to simmer, and cook, uncovered, for 1 hour. Add a small amount of water, if needed. To serve, cover 2 cookie sheets with tortilla chips. Spoon on the meat sauce, and top with any or all of the toppings.

It really DOES look like a Tijuana Train Wreck. A little bit of everything scattered all over the top. Ahhh, but the taste is no accident!

Tom's Terrific Tamale Pie

2 lbs. lean ground chuck or round	2 (16-oz.) cans tomatoes, undrained and mashed
2 medium onions, diced	2 tablespoons plain flour
1 small green pepper, diced	1-1/2 cups plain yellow corn meal
1 (4-oz.) can chopped green chilies	1-1/2 cups cold tap water
5 tablespoons chili powder	3 cups boiling water
3 teaspoons salt, divided	2 cups grated sharp Cheddar cheese
1 (4-oz.) can black olives, chopped	

Follow order of instructions exactly. Prepare a shallow 9- x 13-inch baking dish with spray-oil. In a skillet, cook ground beef with onions; then add green pepper, green chilies, chili powder, 1-1/2 teaspoon of salt, black olives, and tomatoes. Bring to a boil; then reduce heat and simmer, uncovered, for 30 minutes. Stir in flour, and cook 1 minute. In a medium saucepan, stir together the corn meal, the remaining 1-1/2 teaspoons of the salt, and the cold water. Add the boiling water; then cook and stir constantly until the mixture is thick, about 5 minutes. Quickly spread corn meal mixture to cover bottom of the dish; then press mixture up the sides of dish like a pie crust. Finally, press bottom mixture to form a solid crust. Carefully spoon meat mixture, avoiding any grease, on bottom of crust, and spread to cover. Sprinkle the grated cheese evenly over top. Bake at 350 degrees for 50 minutes. As soon as pie is removed from oven, place a double layer of clean paper towel on top to blot any extra oil from cheese; then discard paper towel. Allow to cool for about 8 to 10 minutes before cutting into squares to serve.

My father, Thomas Carter Sparks, Sr., or Tom, or Tommy, as he was affectionately known in these parts, was a "chef." Not by profession but by avocation. He loved to create new recipes, and he and my mother entertained often. Their parties were always fun and "the place to be"! Fortunately, my mother continues the tradition with possibly a little heavenly help!

Thai Beef and Celery

1-1/2 lbs. ground round	1/4 teaspoon crushed red pepper
10 ribs celery with leafy tops, washed and strings removed	5 tablespoons Worcestershire sauce
1 large onion, sliced in rings	3 tablespoons soy sauce
1 clove garlic, minced	Hot white rice
1 teaspoon garlic salt	

In skillet, stir-fry beef until browned; drain. Cut celery and leaves diagonally. Add celery, onion rings, and garlic; continue stir-frying until vegetables soften. Sprinkle with garlic salt and crushed red pepper; then mix. Stir in Worcestershire sauce and soy sauce; continue to stir-fry until vegetables are tender-crisp. Serve over hot white rice. Serves 4.

The recipe was given to my parents Gene and Tommy Sparks many years ago by a gentleman from Thailand visiting our country. Wonder where he is now? I doubt that it would ever have occurred to him that his recipe would be used in an American cookbook! Small world we live in . . .

Melissa's Crockpot Taco Dinner

2 lbs. lean ground beef	1 (15-oz.) can pinto beans
1 (1-1/4-oz.) package dry taco seasoning mix	1 (15-oz.) can kidney beans
4 oz. package dry Ranch Dressing	2 cups chopped onions
1 (16-oz.) can whole kernel corn	1 (4-oz.) can chopped green chilies
	4 (16-oz.) cans diced tomatoes

Cook and drain beef. Combine beef and remaining ingredients in a large bowl; mix well. Pour soup to fill line in crockpot; freeze extra soup. Cover crockpot and simmer on high for 5 hours or on low for 7 to 8 hours.

Makes quite a large portion of soup. Melissa Ellis could feed all of Fort Deposit with this recipe! It is delicious and such an easy meal for a casual crowd. Freezes well.

South of the Border Supper

1-1/2 lbs. lean ground beef	2 (10-oz.) packages frozen
1/4 cup chopped onions	chopped spinach
1 (1-1/4-oz.) package dry taco	1 teaspoon salt
seasoning mix	3 cups grated Monterey Jack
1 cup water	cheese, divided
1 (16-oz.) jar mild taco	2 cups diced cooked ham
sauce, divided	1-1/2 cups sour cream
6 to 8 flour or corn tortillas	Paprika

Brown and drain the ground beef; then add onions, and cook until onions are soft. Stir in the dry taco seasoning mix and the water; simmer for 10 minutes. Prepare a 9- x 13-inch baking dish with spray-oil; then pour 1/2 of the mild taco sauce into the bottom. Place 3 or 4 tortillas on the sauce for 1 minute; then turn the tortillas. Cut tortillas to make a full layer. Cook the spinach and salt in the amount of water called for on the spinach package; then drain until very dry. Stir 1/2 of the drained spinach in beef mixture, and spread the mixture on the tortillas. Sprinkle with 1/2 of the cheese. Place the remaining tortillas on top of the cheese; then pour on the remaining mild taco sauce. Add the ham in a layer, and spread the sour cream over the entire top. Scatter the remaining spinach over the sour cream; then sprinkle with the remaining cheese. Cover and bake at 350 degrees for 25 minutes; then uncover, sprinkle with paprika, and continue to bake an additional 25 minutes. Allow to cool for 10 minutes before cutting into squares.

Ugly and delicious!

Barbecued Hamburger Biscuits

This recipe is popular and may need to be doubled. It can also be used as an after-school snack or as a traveling breakfast.

3/4 lb. lean ground chuck or round	1 tablespoon soy sauce
1/4 teaspoon salt	1 teaspoon brown sugar
1/2 cup catsup	1 tablespoon minced onion
1/4 teaspoon garlic salt	1 can refrigerator biscuits
1 tablespoon vinegar	Grated Cheddar cheese

Preheat oven to 400 degrees. In a skillet, cook ground beef until done; drain the beef, and add salt. In a small bowl, mix the catsup, garlic salt, vinegar, soy sauce, brown sugar, and onion. Stir the catsup mixture into the beef, and mix well. Prepare muffin tins with spray-oil. Press a single biscuit in a muffin cup, and form the biscuit into a cup; repeat with all biscuits. Spoon the beef mixture into the biscuit cups, and top with cheese. Bake the biscuits in the preheated oven for 10 to 12 minutes.

Kids love to "help" make this recipe. They especially like pressing the biscuits into the muffin cups to make the biscuit cups. Be sure to "strong-arm" them into washing their hands before "helping." Otherwise you may have tiny dark fingerprints on the biscuit cups!

Taco Salad in Corn Tortilla Cups

1 dozen 6-inch corn tortillas
20-oz. ground round
1-1/4 teaspoons salt
1/2 teaspoon ground cumin
2 tablespoons chili powder
1 cup diced fresh tomatoes
4 oz. Monterey Jack cheese,
   finely grated

4 oz. sharp Cheddar cheese,
   finely grated
1/2 cup chopped green onions,
   with tops
Paprika
6 cups shredded lettuce

Salad Dressing:

1/2 avocado, peeled and
   chopped
1 small onion, quartered

1 (4-oz.) can chopped
   green chilies
3/4 cup buttermilk
1/4 teaspoon salt
1/2 teaspoon liquid red hot
   sauce (not Tabasco)

Preheat oven to 400 degrees. Fit the tortillas into spray-oil prepared large muffin tins to form the tortilla cups. Some brands of tortillas do not fit too well and look like funnels instead of cups; no problem! Bake for 5 minutes; then remove from the oven, and allow to completely cool. In a skillet, cook the beef until done; drain and crumble. Sprinkle with salt, cumin, and chili powder. Heat beef and spices while stirring for 1 minute; then immediately mix in the tomatoes, both cheeses, and green onions; set aside. In a food processor or blender, combine and blend all salad dressing ingredients. Fill each tortilla cup 1/2 full of the cooked beef mixture, and top each with 2 tablespoons of the salad dressing. Garnish with paprika sprinkled on top. Put 1 cup shredded lettuce on each of 6 dinner plates. Make a hole in the center of the lettuce, and place 2 filled tortillas cups. Serve extra salad dressing on the side for the lettuce. Serves 6.

Crazy Casserole

1-1/2 lbs. lean ground beef	1 cup ricotta or cottage cheese
28 oz. spaghetti sauce	2 eggs, well beaten
(homemade or prepared)	1-1/4 cups grated
1 (4-oz.) can chopped	Cheddar cheese
green chilies	1-1/4 cups grated Monterey
1 (1-1/4-oz.) package dry taco	Jack cheese
seasoning mix	6 to 8 flour or corn tortillas

In a large skillet, cook the ground beef, and drain. Add the spaghetti sauce, green chilies, and dry taco seasoning mix; blend well. Bring the mixture to a boil; then reduce heat to simmer, uncovered, for 10 minutes. In a small bowl, combine ricotta cheese and the well beaten eggs. Mix the grated Cheddar and Monterey Jack cheeses together. Prepare a 9- x 13-inch baking dish with spray-oil. Make 2 layers of all of the ingredients. Begin with 1/2 of the meat, 1/2 of the tortillas, 1/2 of the ricotta, and 1/2 of the grated cheeses; repeat the layers. Bake, uncovered, at 350 degrees for 30 minutes. Allow to stand and cool for 10 minutes before cutting into squares to serve. Serves 6 to 8.

Definitely a "crazy" casserole since it is both a little Mexican and a little Italian. Actually, I suppose it is really a North American creation because it's a beautiful blend of many things.

Quick Southwestern Chili

1-1/2 lbs. ground chuck	1 (1-1/4-oz.) package dry
or round	taco mix
1 large onion, chopped	1 (1-oz.) package dry Ranch
2 (28-oz.) cans diced tomatoes	Salad Dressing mix
2 (15-oz.) cans pinto beans	Tortilla chips
1 (4-oz.) can chopped	Grated sharp Cheddar cheese
green chilies	

In a Dutch oven, brown the ground beef and onion; drain well. Add all remaining ingredients, except chips and cheese, and simmer for 20 minutes. Serve over tortilla chips, and top with cheese.

Poultry

Golden Puffed Chicken

1 sheet of a (17-1/4-oz.) package of puff pastry, thawed	1 egg, well beaten
2 tablespoons margarine	1 tablespoon water
4 boneless, skinless chicken breast halves	4 oz. cream cheese and chive ready-made dip
Salt and pepper	4 tablespoons real bacon bits (no soy bean substitutes)

Unfold pastry, and allow to begin to thaw. Preheat oven to 400 degrees. In a large skillet, melt the margarine over medium-high heat, and cook the chicken breasts until browned on both sides. Salt and pepper on both sides as desired. Remove the chicken to a plate; cover and refrigerate for a minimum of 15 minutes or as long as 24 hours. When ready to cook, use a small bowl to beat the egg and water together; set aside. Place the thawed pastry on a lightly floured board and roll out to a 14-inch square. Divide the square into 4 smaller equal squares of 7-inches each. Spread the center of each square, where the chicken will be placed, with 2 tablespoons of the cream cheese and chive dip. Sprinkle with 1 tablespoon of the bacon bits, and place the cooled chicken breast on top; repeat with all squares. Brush the edges of the squares with the egg mixture. Fold each corner to the center on top of the chicken, and seal the edges. Prepare a flat baking pan with spray-oil, and place the 4 squares on the pan with the seam sides down. Brush the top and sides with the egg mixture. Bake in the preheated oven for 25 minutes or until golden brown. Serves 4.

Mike's Marinated Chicken Breasts for the Grill

Marinate 8 hours or overnight.

1/2 cup unsweetened white
   grape juice
1/4 cup dry white wine
1/4 cup soy sauce

1 tablespoon sesame seeds
1/4 teaspoon garlic powder
2 tablespoons vegetable oil
1/4 teaspoon ground ginger
4 to 6 boneless, skinless chicken
   breast halves

Mix all ingredients except chicken breasts in a bowl until well blended. Place the chicken breasts in a shallow glass baking dish, and pour on the marinade. Cover dish, and allow to marinate in the refrigerator at least 8 hours or overnight. Turn the chicken breasts in the marinade several times to marinate evenly. Grill over medium heat until the breasts are completely cooked but not dried out. Serves 3 to 6.

Mike Presley is a wizard at the grill! You won't believe your taste buds on this one. It is truly out-of-this-world.

Grilled Garlic Lime Chicken

1/2 cup soy sauce
1/4 cup lime juice
1 tablespoon Worcestershire
   sauce
2 cloves garlic, minced

1/2 teaspoon dry mustard
1/2 teaspoon coarsely ground
   black pepper
4 boneless, skinless chicken
   breast halves

In a large bowl, mix all the ingredients except the chicken. Add the chicken to the sauce, and turn to coat. Cover and marinate in the refrigerator for 30 minutes; then discard the marinade. Grill chicken over hot coals for about 6 minutes per side or until done.

chicken Yum-Yum

1/4 cup plain flour	1/4 cup vegetable oil
3 teaspoons salt, plus extra, divided	4 green onions, chopped with tops
1/4 teaspoon fresh, coarsely ground black pepper	3/4 cup sliced fresh mushrooms
Dash of thyme	2 tablespoons lemon juice
6 chicken breast halves	1 teaspoon granulated sugar
	1/3 cup cranberry or apple juice

In a clean plastic bag, mix the flour, 2 teaspoons of the salt, pepper, and thyme. Place washed and patted-dry chicken breast halves in the plastic bag, and shake to coat each piece. In a large skillet, heat the oil, and pan-fry both sides of the chicken breasts until browned. Sprinkle with a little extra salt. Add green onions and mushrooms to the skillet; cover and simmer for 3 minutes. Prepare a shallow 2-quart baking dish with spray-oil. Place browned chicken breast halves in the baking dish. In a small bowl, mix lemon juice, sugar, the remaining 1 teaspoon salt, and juice. Pour the juice mixture over the chicken. Bake, uncovered, at 325 degrees for 35 to 45 minutes. Serves 3 to 6.

chicken Tuxedo

6 boneless, skinless chicken breast halves	Soft cream cheese
	Strawberry preserves
Salt and pepper	3 bacon strips, halved

Pound the chicken breasts until flat; then lightly sprinkle with salt and pepper on both sides. On the side of the chicken breast that is less smooth, spread 1 teaspoon of cream cheese over the entire surface. Place 1/2 teaspoon of the preserves on the cream cheese, and spread. Roll the chicken breast, and secure with a toothpick. Stretch 1/2 strip of bacon tightly around the chicken roll, and secure with toothpicks. Prepare a 2-quart baking dish with spray-oil. Place chicken rolls in the dish, and bake at 350 degrees for about 1 hour. Place under broiler to finish browning the tops for 5 minutes at 500 degrees.

Parmesan Chicken Roll-ups

6 to 12 boneless, skinless chicken breast fillets or tenderloins 1 clove garlic, finely minced 2 tablespoons lemon juice 1/4 cup margarine, melted 1/2 cup grated Parmesan cheese	1/2 cup Italian dry bread crumbs 1 teaspoon salt 1 teaspoon freshly ground black pepper Garnish: paprika and/or dried parsley flakes

Wash and drain the chicken. In a small bowl, combine garlic, lemon juice, and melted margarine. In a medium bowl, mix cheese, crumbs, salt, and pepper. Dip chicken into margarine mixture; then roll in crumb mixture to coat. Roll chicken up, and secure with a toothpick. Prepare a shallow baking dish with spray-oil. Place the chicken roll-ups in the dish. Drizzle with the remaining margarine mixture, and sprinkle with a little paprika and/or parsley to garnish. Cover with aluminum foil, and bake at 350 degrees for 40 minutes; then uncover and bake for 10 to 20 minutes longer depending on the size of the roll-ups. Check chicken for doneness, since the number of roll-ups will vary and may require longer baking. Garnish.

An ideal special occasion recipe since it can be expanded if needed and gives you specific numbers of servings. Figure on about 2 roll-ups per person, if there are equal numbers of men and women guests. The women may eat less and the men may eat more or possibly vice versa!

Baked Chicken Nuggets

1/2 cup fine dry bread crumbs 1/4 cup grated Parmesan cheese 1/4 teaspoon salt 1/2 teaspoon dried whole basil	1/2 teaspoon dried whole thyme 4 chicken breast halves, skinned and boned 1/4 cup margarine, melted

Combine first 5 ingredients in a plastic bag; shake well. Cut chicken into 1-inch pieces; dip chicken pieces in margarine, and shake a few at a time in bread crumb mixture. Place on a lightly greased baking sheet. Bake at 400 degrees for 20 minutes or until tender and done. Serves 4.

Apple-Pecan Stuffed Chicken Breasts

6 boneless, skinless chicken breast halves, salted 1-1/2 cups finely diced Granny Smith apples	1/4 cup golden seedless raisins 1/4 cup chopped pecans 3 tablespoons minced onion

Apple Glaze: 1/4 cup orange juice concentrate	1/4 cup margarine 1/4 cup apple jelly 1/4 cup dry sherry

Pound chicken breast halves to 1/4-inch thickness. In a medium bowl, combine apples, raisins, pecans, and onions; mix well. Place spoonful of stuffing on each chicken breast, dividing evenly. Roll breast, and tuck in sides; then secure with toothpicks. Prepare a 2-quart baking dish with spray-oil. Bake, uncovered, at 350 degrees for 45 minutes. Brush frequently with apple glaze. To make apple glaze, place all glaze ingredients into a small saucepan. Bring to a boil; then simmer for 2 to 3 minutes.

Pecan Crunch Chicken

1 egg 1 cup evaporated milk 1 teaspoon salt 1/2 teaspoon ground pepper 1/2 teaspoon garlic salt	1/4 teaspoon Tabasco sauce 1 cup crushed cornflakes 1/2 cup self-rising flour 1/2 cup medium chopped pecans 4 chicken breast halves

In a bowl, use a fork or wisk to beat the egg very well; then beat in the evaporated milk, salt, pepper, garlic salt, and Tabasco. In another bowl, mix the cornflakes, flour, and pecans. Dip the chicken breasts in the egg mixture; then roll in the pecan mixture to coat. Fry in vegetable oil until breasts are done and crispy. Drain on paper towels.

Teriyaki Grilled Chicken Breasts

Marinate for 4 hours.	1/3 cup Kikkoman Teriyaki Baste & Glaze
	1 large clove garlic, minced
4 to 8 chicken breast halves	1 tablespoon chopped green onions with tops
1 tablespoon soy sauce	2 teaspoons toasted sesame seeds
1 tablespoon dry sherry	

Wash chicken, and pat dry. In a glass bowl, mix all ingredients except chicken and sesame seeds. Place chicken in marinade, and turn to coat; cover and refrigerate for 4 hours. Turn chicken several times. When ready to cook, remove chicken from marinade to plate, and sprinkle with sesame seeds. Place chicken on a medium low-heat grill, and grill slowly with the cover down. Turn several times during grilling. Before removing the chicken from the grill, check for doneness throughout. Immediately salt and pepper the chicken breasts after removing from the grill.

Plum Good Chicken

3 lbs. chicken pieces	1/4 cup orange juice
1/2 cup soy sauce	1 clove garlic, minced
1/2 cup plum jam	Paprika
1/4 cup honey	

Arrange chicken, skin side down, in a shallow 9- x 13-inch, foil-lined baking pan. In a small bowl, combine soy sauce, jam, honey, orange juice, and garlic. Brush chicken generously with some of the mixture; then pour remaining sauce over the chicken. Cover and bake at 350 degrees for 25 minutes; then uncover and turn chicken pieces. Continue to cook, uncovered, for 30 minutes longer; baste occasionally. After the 30 minutes cooking time, sprinkle with paprika, and cook an additional 15 minutes. Serves 4 to 6.

Light Chicken Alfredo

1/4 cup liquid Butter Buds or 1 tablespoon margarine	1/4 cup light Parmesan cheese
1/4 cup plain flour	4 boneless, skinless chicken breast halves, cooked, salted, and chopped
1 cup evaporated skim milk	
3/4 to 1 cup chicken broth, skimmed of fat	1 (8-oz.) can sliced mushrooms, drained
1/4 teaspoon minced garlic	12 oz. fettuccine
1/4 teaspoon salt	Fresh chopped parsley
1/2 teaspoon freshly ground black pepper	

In a large skillet over low heat, blend the liquid Butter Buds or margarine into the flour; then gradually stir in the skim milk and chicken broth, keeping the mixture smooth. Add garlic, salt, and pepper. Continue to cook over low heat, stirring constantly, until sauce thickens. Stir in the Parmesan cheese until blended. Add the cooked chicken and mushrooms; cook 3 minutes, and set aside. Cook the fettuccine according to package directions in salted water; do not overcook. Drain pasta, but do not rinse. While pasta is draining, heat the chicken mixture until very hot; then gently fold in the cooked pasta. If sauce is too thick, add a small amount of evaporated skim milk and chicken broth. Serve hot immediately, sprinkled with the parsley to garnish. Serves 3 to 4.

Greek Pasta

4 chicken breast halves, partially frozen	1 medium sweet red pepper, cut in thin strips
2 tablespoons olive oil	8 oz. angel hair pasta
4 oz. fresh mushrooms, sliced	1/2 teaspoon salt
1 unpeeled small zucchini, cut into match-stick-size strips	3 to 4 oz. feta cheese, crumbled

Cut chicken breasts in thin strips; saute in olive oil until done. Stir in mushrooms, zucchini, pepper strips, and cook until vegetables are tender-crisp. Cook pasta in boiling salted water for 3 to 4 minutes; drain immediately, do not overcook! Bring chicken mixture a high temperature; add drained pasta, and toss gently. Sprinkle with the salt, and toss to mix; then add crumbled feta cheese, and continue to toss until cheese is completely melted and blended. Serve immediately. Serves 4 to 6.

Great Chicken Pizza

2 boneless, skinless chicken breast halves	1 small to medium sweet red pepper, sliced thin
Salt to taste	1/2 to 1 small green pepper, sliced thin
Ground cumin	8 oz. sharp Cheddar cheese, grated
Freshly ground black pepper	8 oz. Provolone cheese, grated
Barbecue sauce (homemade or already prepared)	8 oz. Muenster cheese, grated
1 baked pizza crust	
1 small to medium onion, sliced thin	

Preheat oven to 375 degrees. Cut chicken into thin strips. Sprinkle the strips with salt, cumin, and black pepper. Saute the strips in a skillet with a little of the barbecue sauce until done; do not overcook. When chicken is cooked, spread the pizza crust liberally with some of the barbecue sauce. Place all ingredients on pizza crust, and bake in the preheated oven until cheeses are melted. Remove and allow to sit 5 minutes before cutting.

Cajun "Drunk" Chicken

1 whole (2-1/2 to 3 lb.) chicken fryer	Garlic salt
1 (12-oz.) can Budweiser beer, room temperature	Onion salt
4 oz. liquid crab boil	Celery salt
	Cayenne pepper

Clean the fryer cavity, and wash inside and outside; then place on paper towels to drain. Open the beer, and pour 1/2 of it into a glass. Drink or discard (you gotta be kiddin'.) Pour the crab boil into the remaining beer in the can. Season the entire fryer both inside and outside generously with the garlic salt, onion salt, celery salt, and a smaller amount of cayenne pepper (powerful stuff!) Insert the beer can with the opened top "up" into the fryer cavity. Heat the grill to medium on ONE SIDE ONLY; then place the fryer and the can on the unheated side of the grill using the fryer legs as part of a tripod effect along with the can to make the fryer stand vertically. Cover grill, and cook slowly for 1-3/4 to 2 hours.

Cajun friends of Cemira Price taught her how to cook this fabulous chicken. It can also be cooked, uncovered, on a baking pan in the same way in a 350 degree oven for the same amount of time. Check the chicken fairly often since it does get "drunk" and can fall over. Now that tragedy could force you to open another beer and force you to drink another 1/2 of it to replace the fallen one! Mercy, mercy what a shame! Nonetheless, the chicken will be "right some good."

Sit Down chicken

1 (3 to 3-1/2 lb.) chicken fryer	Lemon pepper marinade
Salt	Paprika

Place whole chicken with breast side up in a spray-oil prepared 2-quart baking dish with nothing on it and no liquid added. Bake at 350 degrees for 2 hours. Remove from oven, and immediately sprinkle with salt and lemon pepper marinade, outside and inside the chicken cavity; then sprinkle the outside with a good bit of paprika. The hot poultry will draw in the spices. Serve while hot. Serves 4 to 6.

What an easy way to cook. Wash the chicken, put it in the pan, begin baking, and go sit down! Let it cook itself.

Hindes' Overton Lamb Roast

3-1/2 lbs. lamb shank roast	3 tablespoons lemon juice
1 partial jar of commercially prepared minced garlic	1-1/2 teaspoons nutmeg
	3 tablespoons light brown sugar
6 tablespoons Grey Poupon mustard	Salt
6 tablespoons balsamic vinegar	Fresh, coarsely ground black pepper

Remove all membrane and skin from lamb; then wash. Pierce holes in lamb with a knife, and twist knife to enlarge holes. Partially fill holes with some of the garlic. Preheat oven to 500 degrees. In a small saucepan combine mustard, vinegar, lemon juice, nutmeg, and brown sugar. Bring to a boil; then reduce heat to simmer for 5 minutes. Brown roast in the oven on all sides; then salt and pepper entire roast. Drizzle hot sauce over roast; and reduce oven heat to 325 degrees. Cook lamb for about 2 hours, baste every 20 minutes, until meat is done and lightly crusted on the outside. Serves 6.

Mitzie and Jack Hinde from Birmingham, Alabama, are old and dear friends. They have served me this wonderful lamb roast on many occasions. Jack cooks it; and Mitzie and I graciously chow down on the scrumptious creation!

Turkey or Chicken Tenderloin Kabobs

Marinate overnight.

1 or 2 turkey tenderloins or
   several chicken breast fillets
1 (20-oz.) can pineapple chunks,
   liquid reserved
2/3 cup soy sauce

2 tablespoons cooking sherry
1/2 teaspoon ground ginger
1 large clove garlic, crushed
Vegetables of choice for kabobs,
   i.e. onions, green peppers,
   cherry tomatoes, squash,
   sweet red peppers, etc.

Cut meat into large cubes. In a glass bowl combine pineapple juice, soy sauce, cooking sherry, ginger, and garlic; mix well. Place meat cubes and pineapple chunks in marinade, and stir. Cover and marinate overnight in refrigerator. When ready to cook, thread meat cubes, pineapple chunks, and vegetables on skewers; discard marinade. Grill over low heat, turning often; for 12 to 15 minutes. Meat should be thoroughly cooked but not dried out.

Chicken Hong Kong

Marinate overnight.

8 chicken thighs or 1 cut-up
   chicken fryer
Juice from 1 fresh lime
3/4 cup soy sauce
2 cloves garlic, minced

1/3 cup frozen limeade,
   undiluted
1 tablespoon ground ginger
1/4 teaspoon white or
   black pepper
1 fresh lime, sliced thin, divided

Wash chicken, leaving skin on one side, and blot with paper towel. Place chicken in a glass bowl, and squeeze lime juice over chicken; set aside for 15 minutes. In a small bowl, mix remaining ingredients and 1/2 the lime slices. Pour marinade over chicken, turning pieces several times; cover and refrigerate overnight. When time to cook, place chicken, skin side down, in a baking dish; cover with marinade. Bake, uncovered, at 350 degrees for 35 minutes; then turn chicken, and continue baking, uncovered, for another 40 minutes. Pour off marinade. Garnish with remaining fresh lime slices.

Oriental Baked Chicken with Noodles

2 to 3 lbs. chicken pieces	1/4 teaspoon garlic powder
1/3 cup soy sauce	1/4 teaspoon poultry seasoning
2 tablespoons lemon juice	Paprika
1/4 teaspoon onion powder	1 (8-oz.) package wide noodles

Prepare a 9- x 13-inch baking dish with spray-oil. Place the chicken pieces with the skin side down in the pan. In a small bowl, mix the soy sauce, lemon juice, onion powder, garlic powder, and poultry seasonings; pour over the chicken pieces. Sprinkle liberally with paprika; then cover the dish tightly with aluminum foil. Bake at 350 degrees for 1 hour and 15 minutes. Baste once during the cooking time; then replace the foil cover. Shortly before the end of the chicken cooking time, cook the noodles according to package directions to be done about 8 minutes before chicken has finished cooking. Drain noodles; then place in a medium bowl, and pour enough of the cooked chicken liquid over the noodles to add flavor; do not use all of the liquid. Serve hot chicken over the hot noodles.

Cajun Barbecue Sauce

1 cup margarine (2 sticks)	3 cloves garlic, minced
1 cup Worcestershire sauce	3 tablespoons brown sugar
1 cup white vinegar	1 large onion, diced
2 tablespoons lemon juice	Tabasco sauce to taste
1 teaspoon dry mustard	

In a heavy saucepan, mix all ingredients; bring to a boil. Cover and simmer for 30 minutes.

This is "great on yo' slow-cooked chicken."

Puttin' on the Ritz

3 stacks Ritz crackers, keep sealed in packages	1 (10-3/4 oz.) can golden mushroom soup
2-1/2 cups cooked, chopped, salted chicken	16 oz. shredded mozzarella cheese
8 oz. sour cream	Paprika

Prepare a 9- x 13-inch baking dish with spray-oil. Keeping the bag sealed, crush each of the Ritz cracker stacks to make crumbs. Sprinkle 1 bag of the crushed Ritz crackers in the bottom of the baking dish. In a large bowl, mix all of the remaining ingredients except Ritz crackers and paprika until well blended. Make layers of 1/2 chicken mixture, 1 more bag Ritz cracker crumbs; then repeat the layers. Sprinkle with paprika to garnish. Bake, uncovered, at 350 degrees for 40 to 50 minutes until bubbly. Serves 6 to 8.

Aunt Betty Hooper Green gave this recipe for the Priester's Pecan Company cookbook, and our taste buds thank her. It is absolutely divine to be so simple. Crushing the bags of Ritz is kind of fun! I guess it brings out the child in me, which is never very far below the surface . . .

Beth's Magic Chicken Pie

3 to 4 cups cooked, chopped, salted chicken	11 oz. chicken broth
2 hard-boiled eggs, sliced thin	1 cup self-rising flour
1 (10-3/4 oz.) can cream of chicken soup	1 cup milk
	6 tablespoons margarine, melted

Prepare a 2-1/2-quart baking dish with spray-oil. Make layers, beginning with the chopped chicken, then the sliced eggs. In a medium bowl, mix together the chicken soup and the chicken broth. Spoon on the soup mixture as the third layer, and spread to cover. Using the same bowl, blend the remaining ingredients, and pour on as the fourth layer. Bake, uncovered, at 400 degrees for 30 to 40 minutes. Serves 6.

Juliet's Chicken Almond Casserole

10 tablespoons margarine
1/2 cup chopped onion
8 oz. fresh mushrooms, sliced
1/2 cup plain flour
2-1/2 cups Half and Half
4 cups chicken broth
2 cups grated sharp Cheddar
   cheese

1/4 teaspoon salt
1/2 teaspoon freshly ground
   black pepper
2 teaspoons lemon juice
6 oz. flat egg noodles, cooked
   and drained
6 cups cooked, chopped,
   salted chicken

Topping:

2 cups grated sharp Cheddar
   cheese

3/4 cup slivered almonds

In a large skillet, melt margarine, and saute onions until soft. Add mushrooms; then slowly blend in the flour until smooth. Gradually stir in Half and Half, keeping the mixture smooth. Stir in chicken broth, and cook over medium heat until thickened. Add grated cheese, salt, pepper, and lemon juice. Stir and heat until cheese is melted. Turn heat to simmer, and cook, uncovered, 10 to 15 minutes. Add noodles and chicken; mix. Prepare a shallow 9- x 13-inch baking dish with spray-oil. Pour chicken mixture into baking dish. Top with grated cheese and almonds. Bake at 350 degrees for 1 hour.

Southern Escalloped Chicken

1/2 cup margarine, divided and melted	1 cup milk
1/2 cup plain flour	1 cup Half and Half
3/4 teaspoon salt, divided	4 cups crumbled corn bread, lightly packed in cup
3/4 teaspoon freshly ground black pepper, divided	1 cup finely chopped celery
3-1/4 cups chicken broth	1 small onion, finely chopped
	4 to 5 cups cooked, sliced chicken

Prepare a shallow 9- x 13-inch baking dish with spray-oil. In a large skillet, melt 1/4 cup of the margarine, and stir in the flour until smooth. Add 1/2 teaspoon of the salt and 1/4 teaspoon of the black pepper; then gradually stir in the chicken broth, keeping the mixture smooth. Heat and stir in the milk and Half and Half until mixture slightly thickens. In a large bowl, mix the crumbled corn bread with the celery, onion, and remaining salt, pepper, and melted margarine; mix to blend all ingredients. Pour the milk mixture in the corn bread mixture; blend well. Place the chicken in the bottom of the baking dish; then pour the corn bread mixture over the top. Cover and bake at 350 degrees for 1 hour; then uncover and cook an additional 15 minutes. Serves 8.

Tetrazzini

This recipe can be made with either turkey or chicken.

1/2 cup chopped onion
1/2 cup chopped celery
1/4 cup margarine
1 (10-3/4-oz.) can chicken broth
8 oz. cream cheese, cubed
8 oz. spaghetti, cooked, salted, and drained

3 to 4 cups turkey or chicken, cooked, salted, and chopped
1 (4-oz.) can chopped mushrooms, drained
2 tablespoons chopped pimentos
1/4 teaspoon salt
1/4 cup grated Parmesan cheese
Paprika

Saute onion, celery, and margarine. Add broth and cream cheese; then stir over low heat until cheese is melted. Add remaining ingredients except Parmesan and paprika; then mix gently. Prepare a 9- x 13-inch baking dish with spray-oil. Spread the pasta mixture in the baking dish, and sprinkle with the Parmesan cheese and paprika. Bake at 350 degrees for 30 minutes or until bubbly. Serves 6 to 8.

White Barbecue Sauce

Use this sauce to baste chicken, pork, or ribs

1 pint mayonnaise
2 tablespoons pepper

1 tablespoon salt
6 tablespoons lemon juice
6 tablespoons white vinegar
4 tablespoons granulated sugar

In a medium saucepan, mix ingredients until smooth. Use as a basting sauce while cooking meat on grill. Sauce will keep refrigerated several weeks in a tightly covered glass or plastic container.

chicken Sorrento

4 cups cooked penne pasta
  (cook pasta as instructed
  below; then measure the
  cooked pasta)
1 tablespoon olive oil, plus extra
  for tossing in pasta
1 or 2 (10-oz.) packages frozen
  asparagus, thawed
1 (4-oz.) can chopped mushrooms
2 tablespoons chopped pimento or
  fresh sweet red pepper

2 cups cooked, chopped,
  salted chicken
1/3 cup cooked, crumbled bacon
1/4 cup dry white wine
1/4 cup chicken broth
1/4 cup Parmesan cheese
1/4 to 1/2 teaspoon salt
1/4 teaspoon freshly ground
  black pepper
Paprika

In a Dutch oven, cook the pasta in salted water according to the package directions; do not overcook! Drain the pasta immediately after cooking, and place the drained pasta back in the Dutch oven. Add a small amount of olive oil to the pasta, and toss to coat. Slice the thawed asparagus into 1/2-inch pieces. In a large skillet, heat 1 tablespoon of the olive oil, and saute the asparagus, mushrooms, pimentos or sweet red pepper and, chicken for 2 minutes. Add the sauteed mixture to the pasta, along with the bacon, wine, and chicken broth. Heat and blend; then sprinkle with cheese, salt, and pepper. Continue to heat, and blend to serving temperature. Sprinkle with paprika at serving time. Serves 2 to 4.

Aztec Cake

1 (16-oz.) can whole tomatoes
4 tablespoons chopped onion
1/4 teaspoon minced garlic
1/2 teaspoon salt
1/2 cup corn oil, divided
1 dozen corn tortillas
3 to 4 cups cooked, chopped,
  salted chicken

Pickled jalapeno pepper slices,
  chopped, to taste
12-oz. mozzarella cheese, grated
4 oz. sour cream
Garnish: grated sharp Cheddar
  cheese

Preheat the oven to 350 degrees. In a food processor or blender, combine the tomatoes, onion, and garlic; blend until smooth. Pour mixture into a medium saucepan; then add the salt and 1/2 teaspoon of the oil. Cook the mixture until it comes to a boil. Prepare a 2-quart round baking dish with spray-oil. Heat the remaining oil until hot, and dip tortillas in the hot oil for a few seconds on each side, just until softened. Drain on paper towels; then dip enough tortillas in the sauce to cover the bottom of the baking dish with 1 layer of tortillas. Sprinkle with chopped chicken, chopped jalapeno pepper slices (suit your own taste), and mozzarella cheese; repeat layers until all tortillas are used. Pour the remaining sauce over the final cheese layer, and spread the sour cream over the entire top. Sprinkle the Cheddar cheese sparsely over the sour cream as garnish. Bake in the preheated oven for only 15 minutes; do not overcook or the tortillas will become too soft. Allow to cool for a few minutes before cutting into wedges.

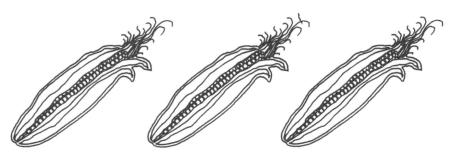

Pork

Jay's Basil and Tomato Pork Chops

Make in advance, if desired.

6 lean pork chops, 1/2-inch thick
Salt and pepper to taste
1 (28-oz.) can diced tomatoes
1 medium onion, sliced in thin
   rings

3 tablespoons Lea and Perrin
   White Wine Worcestershire
   sauce
1/4 teaspoon garlic powder
2 teaspoons crushed basil leaves
1 tablespoon white vinegar
Paprika to sprinkle

Prepare a 9- x 13-inch baking dish with spray-oil. Trim chops of fat. Salt and pepper chops on both sides, and place in baking dish. Drain tomatoes in a small bowl, and reserve liquid. Make a layer of onion rings on top of chops; then a layer of the drained, diced tomatoes. In a medium bowl, mix 2 tablespoons of reserved tomato liquid, white wine Worcestershire sauce, garlic powder, basil leaves, and vinegar until well blended. Pour mixture over chops and vegetables. Cook, uncovered, at 400 degrees for 35 to 45 minutes. Turn once during cooking time, and sprinkle with paprika. Check center of chops for doneness before serving. Serves 3 to 4.

Thomas Jackson Westbrook, or "Jay," is our youngest son, and an outstanding chef. He truly finds cooking to be a relaxing art form. His wife, Melody, and their friends always seem to be willing and enthusiastic cheerleaders of his culinary efforts. I think there's more than just a "chip" off the old block here! He can put me to shame on any recipe, and with mama's blessing.

Grilled Polynesian Pork Chops

Marinate overnight.

6 to 8 pork chops, 1/4 to 1/2-inch thick
1 (20-oz.) can pineapple slices, liquid reserved

2/3 cup soy sauce
2 tablespoons cooking sherry
1/2 teaspoon ground ginger
1 large garlic clove, crushed

Place pork chops in a shallow glass baking dish. In a medium bowl, combine pineapple liquid, soy sauce, cooking sherry, ginger, and garlic; mix well. Pour marinade over pork chops; then place pineapple slices in marinade. Cover and refrigerate overnight; turn chops once. When ready to cook, discard marinade. Grill pork chops and pineapple rings on a medium grill for about 20 to 25 minutes or until chops are thoroughly cooked. Keep pineapple rings on the cooler part of grill to slowly cook until lightly browned and slightly crispy. Serves 4 to 6.

Chinese Sweet and Sour Sausage

1 large onion, sliced in rings
1 large green pepper, sliced in rings
1 large sweet red pepper, sliced in rings
1 tablespoon vegetable oil
1 tablespoon cornstarch
1 teaspoon ground ginger

1 tablespoon rice or other vinegar
1/4 cup red plum jam
3 tablespoons soy sauce
8 oz. smoked link sausage, cooked and sliced
8 oz. pineapple tidbits, drained
Hot, cooked white rice

In a large skillet, saute onion and both peppers in oil for about 5 minutes. In a small bowl, combine cornstarch and ginger; then stir in vinegar. Add jam and soy; blend well. Stir sauce mixture into vegetable mixture, and add cooked sausage and pineapple. Heat on low until thickened, blended, and bubbling. Serve hot over the hot rice. Serves 3 to 4.

Citrus Grilled Pork Chops

Marinate for 6 hours.

4 (6-oz.) lean, loin-cut pork chops
Salt to taste
1 whole lemon rind, grated
   (yellow area only)
1 whole orange rind, grated
   (orange area only)
Juice of the grated orange

Juice of the grated lemon, plus
   extra to make 2 tablespoons
1 tablespoon olive oil
2 tablespoons finely chopped
   green onions with tops
3/4 teaspoon chili powder
1/4 teaspoon paprika
1/4 teaspoon freshly ground
   coarse black pepper
1/4 teaspoon Tabasco sauce

Select a shallow glass baking pan just large enough to fit all chops in one layer. Trim pork chops; then salt and place in pan. In a small bowl, mix rinds, juices, oil, green onion, chili powder, paprika, black pepper, and Tabasco. Pour marinade over chops. Marinate 1 minute; turn chops. Cover and refrigerate 6 hours. At grilling time, remove chops from refrigerator and from marinade; reserve marinade. Cook chops on grill over a medium-high setting; turn after 5 minutes. Brush with reserved marinade, and continue cooking for an additional 7 to 10 minutes or until there is absolutely no pink showing when checked for doneness. Serves 4.

Ham with Strawberry Jam

1/2 cured uncooked ham;
   6 to 8 lbs.
3/4 cup brown sugar, packed
3/4 teaspoon dry mustard

6 tablespoons white vinegar
3 tablespoons soy sauce
3/4 cup strawberry jam or
   preserves

Wash ham and trim all excess fat. In a small bowl, mix all ingredients except ham. Place ham on heavy-duty aluminum foil, and spoon the mixture over the ham. Wrap aluminum foil tightly, and place in a heavy baking pan. Bake at 350 degrees for about 3 hours or until ham tests done. Allow the ham to partially cool before slicing.

Ham and Asparagus Strata

3 medium cooked potatoes, peeled and sliced	1 cup sharp Cheddar cheese, grated
2 (10-oz.) packages frozen asparagus spears	1 uncooked ham steak, 1/2 to 1-inch thick
1/4 cup margarine	1 large onion, sliced thin into rings
1/2 teaspoon salt	Extra salt and pepper
2 tablespoons plain flour	Ritz cracker crumbs
1 cup milk	Paprika

Cook potatoes, or use leftover peeled potatoes. Cook asparagus by package directions in salted water until just tender; drain. In a medium skillet, melt the margarine; add salt and flour, and stir until smooth. Gradually add milk, keeping mixture smooth, and cook until thickened, stirring constantly. Then add cheese, and stir until melted. Cut ham steak into 4 or 6 pieces. Prepare a shallow 9- x 13-inch baking dish with spray-oil. Make layers, beginning with the ham pieces, sliced potatoes, onion rings, a little extra salt and pepper on potatoes and onions, and asparagus spears. Pour sauce over all ingredients; then sprinkle the top with cracker crumbs and paprika. Bake at 350 degrees for 45 minutes. Serves 3 to 4.

A very pretty and colorful strata entree. Two casseroles can be made at the same time for just a few minutes longer preparation time. Cover one casserole with plastic wrap; then cover with aluminum foil and freeze. It will freeze nicely for 3 weeks, and, yes, the potatoes WILL freeze since they are already cooked when you begin this recipe.

Parmesan Mushroom Pork

1 tablespoon plain flour	1/2 cup diced onions
1 tablespoon grated Parmesan cheese	1 clove garlic, minced
1/8 teaspoon freshly ground black pepper	1 cup sliced fresh or canned mushrooms
1/4 teaspoon salt, divided	1/4 teaspoon basil
4 small, lean, boneless pork chops, trimmed	2 tablespoons dry white wine
2 tablespoons olive oil, divided	2 tablespoons water
	1 tablespoon chopped fresh parsley

On sheet of waxed paper, combine flour, Parmesan cheese, pepper, and 1/8 teaspoon of the salt. Dredge both sides of pork chops in flour mixture; reserve remaining flour mixture. In large skillet, heat 1 tablespoon of the olive oil over medium-high heat. Add onions and garlic; then saute until soft. Stir in mushrooms, basil, and remaining 1/8 teaspoon of salt; saute for 1 minute. Remove mushroom mixture to a side plate. Add remaining olive oil to skillet, and heat to medium-high; brown dredged pork chops on both sides; remove pork chops to a side plate. Return mushroom mixture to skillet, and stir in reserved flour mixture. Add wine and water; then heat and stir until thickened. Place pork chops in sauce; cover and simmer for 20 minutes or until thoroughly cooked. Sprinkle with fresh parsley. Serves 2.

Spiced Pork Tenderloin

2 lbs. pork tenderloin	1 tablespoon chili powder
2 teaspoons paprika	1 tablespoon minced garlic
2 teaspoons seasoned salt	

Wash meat, and roll in paper towels. In a small bowl, combine all seasonings. Roll tenderloins in seasonings to coat. Tenderloin may be broiled or grilled. To broil, place meat on a spray-oil prepared baking pan. Broil 5 to 6 inches from heat until no longer pink and cooked throughout, approximately 14 to 16 minutes; turn once. To grill, place on a medium-hot grill for approximately 15 minutes; turn once. Serves 6 to 8.

Quick chops

4 (3/4-inch) pork loin or rib chops, trimmed of fat	4 thin lemon slices
Salt	2 teaspoons brown sugar
4 large thin onion slices	4 tablespoons catsup

Sprinkle both sides of chops with salt. Place chops in a spray-oil prepared 8- x 8-inch baking pan. Top each chop with onion slice, lemon slice, 1/2 teaspoon brown sugar, and 1 tablespoon catsup. Cover and bake at 350 degrees for 30 minutes; uncover, baste, and continue cooking 30 minutes longer. Baste twice more to blend catsup into other juices without actually stirring. Check chops for doneness; there should be no pink area at all. After removing from oven, baste with juices again. Serves 2 to 4.

This is an ideal recipe to let the children help prepare. After preparing the chops and slicing onion and lemon, let the children help "build" the pork chops. You never know, there might be a great chef in the making!

confetti spaghetti

1 tablespoon olive oil	8 oz. fettuccine florentine
2 large onions sliced in rings	1 teaspoon salt
1 bunch green onions, sliced with tops	1 (16-oz.) can small pitted black olives, drained and quartered lengthwise
1 large green pepper, sliced in rings	8 oz. smoked sausage, cooked and sliced
1 large sweet red pepper, sliced in rings	Grated Parmesan or Romano cheese to taste
1 large clove garlic, minced	

In a large skillet or pot, saute in oil all onions, peppers, and garlic until tender. Cook fettuccine by package directions in water with the salt, taking care not to overcook; then drain. Immediately add drained fettuccine to the onion and pepper mixture; then toss gently to blend. Add olives and sausage; toss gently. Sprinkle pasta with cheese to taste. Serves 3 to 4.

Seafood & Fish

Shrimp & Wild Rice by Joan

1-1/2 lbs. small to medium fresh shrimp	1 (8-oz.) can sliced mushrooms, drained
1 (4.5-oz.) box Uncle Ben's Long Grain and Wild Rice	1 (10-3/4-oz.) can cream of chicken soup
1 tablespoon margarine	2 tablespoons Half and Half
1 medium onion, chopped fine	1 tablespoon Worcestershire sauce
1/4 cup chopped green pepper	6 drops Tabasco sauce

Peel shrimp, and rinse in cold water 5 times; then drain. Cook rice by package directions. While rice is cooking, melt margarine in a large skillet, and saute onions and green pepper until limp. Add peeled shrimp, and continue to saute until shrimp are pink in color. Do not overcook! Add mushrooms, and saute 1 minute; then stir and blend in soup, Half and Half, Worcestershire sauce, and Tabasco. Stir in cooked rice until all ingredients are blended. Prepare a shallow, 3-quart baking dish with spray-oil; then pour mixture in baking dish. Bake at 325 degrees for 45 minutes.

The flavor is superb, and preparation is short. My cousin, Joan Backes, of Mobile, Alabama, provided this grand recipe as she has many great recipes in my cookbooks. She entertains with ease and grace, and has few regrets to her invitations to dine!

Lou's Deviled Crab Casserole

1 lb. fresh lump crabmeat (no substitutes)	1 tablespoon finely chopped fresh parsley
Juice of 1 fresh lemon	1/4 teaspoon dry mustard
2 eggs	1/2 cup mayonnaise
1/2 cup margarine	1 tablespoon Worcestershire sauce
1 cup finely chopped onion	4 drops Tabasco sauce
1/2 cup finely chopped green pepper	Ritz crackers
1 cup finely chopped celery	

Place crabmeat in a bowl, sprinkle with the lemon juice, and toss to mix. Hard-boil the eggs; peel and cool. In a skillet, melt the margarine; saute the onion, green pepper, celery, and parsley until very soft. Grate the hard-boiled eggs, and add to the crabmeat; then stir in the sauteed vegetables. Add all remaining ingredients except crackers; mix thoroughly. Prepare a casserole dish with spray-oil; then fill with the crab mixture. (The crab mixture can also be placed in individual ramekins rather than a casserole, if preferred.) Crumble Ritz crackers over the top. Bake at 350 degrees for 30 to 40 minutes.

My favorite aunt, Lucile Judkins Williams, created this deviled crab dish that makes you think you've gone to heaven rather than to the devil!

Charleston Shrimp & Grits

Tasso is spicy ham served in the Charleston area. Substitutes listed below.

Grits:	1/2 teaspoon garlic salt
1 cup quick grits	1/4 teaspoon garlic powder
2 tablespoons margarine	2 eggs, well beaten
1/4 cup milk	1 tablespoon vegetable oil

Sauce:	1/2 cup milk
6 tablespoons margarine, divided	1 lb. small to medium fresh
3 tablespoons plain flour	shrimp, peeled
1/2 teaspoon salt	Salt to taste for shrimp
1/4 teaspoon black pepper	3 oz. diced, cooked tasso,
1/4 teaspoon garlic salt	spicy ham, or spicy link
1/4 teaspoon Tabasco sauce	sausage
1-1/2 cups chicken broth	1/4 cup diced sweet red pepper

Grits: Cook grits by package directions with salt. While grits are cooking, preheat oven to 400 degrees. When grits are cooked, stir in margarine and milk; taste for salt, add if needed. Beat garlic salt and garlic powder in eggs; then beat egg mixture in grits. Prepare a 10-inch iron skillet with spray-oil. Heat vegetable oil in skillet to hot, but not smoking; pour grits mixture in skillet. Place skillet in preheated oven, and bake for 45 minutes, or until browned on edges and top. Remove skillet from oven; set aside, and keep warm.

Sauce: In a large skillet, melt 4 tablespoons of the margarine, and blend in flour until smooth. Add salt, pepper, garlic salt, and Tabasco sauce; then gradually stir in chicken broth, keeping mixture smooth. Stir in milk, and cook until sauce has slightly thickened; set aside. Rinse shrimp in cold water, and drain 5 times. In a medium skillet, melt remaining 2 tablespoons of margarine, and saute drained shrimp until shrimp are pink; do not overcook! Salt shrimp to taste. Add tasso, ham, or sausage, and sweet red pepper. Saute for 1 minute longer. Stir shrimp mixture in sauce, and heat until very hot. Cut warm grits cake into 8 wedges. Serve the hot sauce over grits wedges. Serves 4.

Fabulous, you need to try this!

Rainbow Trout With Brown Butter Pecans

This recipe is a serving for two. It can be adapted to accommodate any number you wish to serve. Figure one trout per person.

2 whole rainbow trout	Coarsely ground black pepper
1/2 fresh lemon	Paprika
Salt	Vegetable oil
Self-rising corn meal	

Sauce:	3/4 cup pecans, coarsely chopped
1/4 lb. butter, softened (no substitutes)	2 tablespoons lemon juice
	Lemon slices or twists to garnish

Rinse the trout under cold water; then place on paper towel, and pat dry. Squeeze the lemon over both sides, and lightly salt whole trout. Spoon corn meal over the fish on both sides to coat. Sprinkle the pepper and paprika on both sides of the trout. In a large skillet, heat a small amount of oil over high heat until it is nearly smoking. Carefully place one trout in the pan, and reduce the heat to medium high. Cook for 3 minutes before turning; then reduce the heat to medium. Cook for an additional 3 minutes or until the trout tests done. Remove to paper towels to drain. Do not cover. Cook remaining trout, and drain.

Sauce: In a medium skillet, melt the softened butter over high heat. Add the pecans, and cook until the butter begins to darken and the nuts start to brown. When the butter stops foaming and begins to clarify, add lemon juice, and blend. Pour the hot sauce over the cooked trout, and garnish with lemon slices or twists. Serves 2.

Crab Au Gratin

1 cup finely chopped onion	1/4 teaspoon black pepper
1/4 cup margarine	1 lb. fresh crabmeat (no substitutes)
1/2 cup plain flour	
5 oz. evaporated milk	8 oz. sharp Cheddar cheese, grated
8 oz. Half and Half	
2 egg yolks	Additional salt to taste, if needed
1/4 teaspoon salt	Paprika

In a large skillet, saute onions in margarine; then blend in flour. Gradually stir in milk, keeping mixture smooth; then stir in Half and Half. Add egg yolks, salt, and both peppers; cook 5 minutes. Add crabmeat and cheese to the skillet, and blend well. Taste for salt, add if needed. Prepare a 1-1/2-quart casserole with spray-oil; spoon the crabmeat mixture in the casserole. Sprinkle the top with paprika, and bake at 375 degrees for 10 to 15 minutes.

Shrimp may be substituted for crabmeat to make Shrimp Au Gratin.

Deviled Oysters

1 pint small fresh oysters	1/4 teaspoon cayenne pepper
1/2 teaspoon garlic powder	1/2 cup self-rising corn meal mix
1/4 teaspoon garlic salt	Vegetable oil
1/4 teaspoon onion salt	

Place oysters in a colander to drain completely. Put all remaining ingredients except the oil in a clean plastic bag; shake to mix. Add oysters to the bag of corn meal mixture, 2 or 3 at a time, and shake to coat completely; coat all oysters. In a small skillet, heat the oil to hot but not smoking; then fry the oysters until brown and done. Drain on paper towel.

This is the best fried oyster recipe I've ever tasted. It gives just the right amount of "devilish" flavor but does not overpower the oyster flavor. No sauce required to enjoy these.

Pickwick Cafe Shrimp

3 to 5 lbs. large fresh shrimp in shells **Water**	**Salt** **12 oz. crab boil**

Sauce:	
1 cup Hellmann's mayonnaise **1 cup chili sauce**	**2 tablespoons tarragon vinegar** **2 tablespoons anchovy paste** **1 teaspoon Tabasco sauce**

Place shrimp in a large container with cold water; then stir with a large spoon, and pour into a colander to drain. Repeat this 5 times; do not cheat! In a large pot, bring to a boil plenty of water that has been salted to taste, plus a little extra salt. Add crab boil; then gently add washed shrimp. Allow shrimp to cook until shells are pink in color; cook an additional 3 to 4 minutes. Immediately remove pot from the heat, and allow to stand for 5 minutes only; then drain all water from the shrimp. Spread the shrimp on cookie sheets to begin cooling. Do not leave shrimp in the pot or in a heap; they will overcook and become mushy. Shrimp can be served warm, room temperature, or chilled. To make sauce, place all ingredients in a medium glass or plastic bowl; stir to blend. Serve room temperature or chilled.

This recipe is an old Montgomery, Alabama, favorite from the Pickwick Cafe on Commerce Street, downtown. It was owned by Mr. Frank Ridolphi, and was THE restaurant of choice. They were famous for the Pickwick Sauce. I was too young, but do you remember?

venetian shrimp & scallops with vermicelli

4 oz. raw vermicelli, broken in half	1 large onion, thinly sliced
Few drops olive oil or melted margarine	10 cherry tomatoes, halved
1/4 cup margarine, or less if desired	4 large fresh mushrooms, sliced
1 small clove garlic, minced	3 tablespoons Parmesan cheese, grated
12 small, tender scallops, halved	1/2 teaspoon salt
8 large raw shrimp, peeled and halved	1/4 teaspoon freshly ground coarse black pepper
	Extra grated Parmesan cheese to sprinkle, if desired

Cook vermicelli in a covered pot in salted boiling water for exactly nine minutes. Immediately drain, and toss with a few drops of olive oil; set aside. Prepare a large skillet with spray-oil. Heat the margarine, and saute the garlic, scallops, shrimp, onions, cherry tomatoes, and mushrooms for 5 minutes or until shrimp are pink. Add the cooked vermicelli, and stir carefully to blend the pasta with the seafood mixture. Continue to heat slowly; then add the Parmesan cheese, salt, and pepper. Gently toss, and turn until all ingredients are mixed and very hot. Serve immediately with extra Parmesan cheese sprinkled on top.

A light seafood pasta, the recipe can be made even lighter by completely eliminating the margarine. You will have to saute a little faster and use a skillet prepared with spray-oil. Bella e deliziosa . . .

David's Crab and Mushroom Mountains

8 oz. large whole fresh white mushrooms, washed	1 clove garlic, finely minced
2 tablespoons margarine	2 tablespoons fresh parsley, finely minced
Salt and pepper to taste	Eggs
1 lb. fresh crabmeat (no substitutes)	Bread crumbs
	Extra butter

Carefully remove stems from the mushroom caps, and chop very fine. In a large skillet, melt the 2 tablespoons margarine, and saute the chopped mushroom stems until tender; salt and pepper to taste. Add enough crabmeat to double the saute mixture. Add garlic and parsley; taste again for salt. Measure mixture, and add one whole beaten egg per cup of crab mixture; blend well. Fill the mushroom caps with the mixture, heaping high like a mountain. Sprinkle tops with bread crumbs, and place a small dot of butter on each mound. Prepare a baking dish with spray-oil; place the stuffed caps in the dish, and bake at 350 degrees for about 15 minutes. Serve hot.

David Rennekamp has provided his mother's recipe, one of his favorites. It can be served as an entree or as an appetizer.

chef Eddie's Oysters

10 oz. small fresh oysters	1/4 cup Italian bread crumbs
1/4 cup grated fresh Parmesan or Romano cheese	3 teaspoons olive oil

Prepare an 8-inch round or square baking dish with spray-oil. Place the well-drained oysters in the dish, and sprinkle with the grated cheese. Then sprinkle the bread crumbs, and drizzle the olive oil over the bread crumbs. Bake at 350 degree for 20 minutes.

Sue and Eddie Pope are both great "chefs." Eddie has kindly contributed this grand oyster dish and the Low Country Boil recipe for you to enjoy. Sue had an experience I'd like to tell that has absolutely nothing to do with cooking, but makes a great story. It seems that when she answered her phone one day, the caller asked to speak to Father Jones. Sue replied, "I'm sorry, you have the wrong number. This is the Pope's residence." The caller replied, "Very funny, Lady!" and hung up in a huff. Sue said it took a couple of minutes before she got the joke and burst into laughter!

capered Red Snapper

1 (1-lb.) fresh red snapper fillet	1 tablespoon lemon juice
Salt	1-1/2 tablespoons margarine
Coarsely ground black pepper	2 teaspoons capers, drained
1/2 fresh lemon	Paprika

Rinse snapper in cold water. Salt and pepper on both sides, and place, skin side down, in a 2-quart baking dish prepared with spray-oil. Squeeze lemon over top of fillet; then pour the lemon juice in the pan. Place bits of margarine over top of fillet. Sprinkle capers over fillet top; then sprinkle with paprika. Bake at 350 degrees for about 20 to 25 minutes. Twice during cooking time, spoon sauce over top of fillet. Snapper is done when fish turns from a transparent white to a solid white and can be flaked with a fork at the thickest part of the fillet. After removing from oven, spoon sauce over top again before serving. Serves 2.

Gary's Favorite Fresh Bass Fillets

Fish must soak for a minimum of 2 hours or overnight.	**Coarsely ground black pepper**
	2 tablespoons vegetable oil
	1 teaspoon celery seed
4 fresh bass fillets	**3 teaspoons Cavender's All**
Salt	**Purpose Greek Seasoning**

Place fillets in a bowl with 1/2 teaspoon salt, and cover fillets with water. Cover bowl, and refrigerate. Before cooking, remove fillets from water, and place on paper towels to drain. Prepare a baking pan with spray-oil, and place fillets in pan; then salt and pepper both sides of fish. Drizzle the vegetable oil over the tops of the fillets; then sprinkle with the celery seed and Cavender's Greek Seasoning. Bake at 350 degrees for about 20 to 25 minutes or until fish flakes and is no longer transparent but solid white in color. Place the pan of fillets under the broiler on 500 degrees just long enough to lightly brown the fillets.

I must mention that this wonderful fish is regularly caught by my newest son, Gary Clements, Genia's husband. He is quite a talented guy, along with having the foresight to marry my daughter. He's a very creative professional illustrator and graphic designer, a fisherman who actually catches fish, Tennessee Walking Horse breeder and rider, downhill skier, guitar player, avid kayaker, and instructor of that sport. This is only the tip of the iceberg of his talents. An all-around nice guy. Genia has developed this great recipe for the bass. The same recipe may be used for other fish such as snapper, grouper, or other thick white fish fillets.

Jo's Barbecued Shrimp

3 to 5 lbs. fresh shrimp, unpeeled	1/4 teaspoon ground rosemary
1/2 lb. butter	2 large fresh lemons, sliced
1/2 lb. margarine	1/2 teaspoon Tabasco sauce
4 tablespoons ground black pepper (yes, tablespoons!)	2 teaspoons salt
	2 cloves garlic, halved
	3 oz. Worcestershire sauce

Place shrimp into a large container with cold water; then stir with a large spoon, and drain in a colander. Repeat 5 times; do not cheat! Preheat oven to 400 degrees. In a medium saucepan, melt butter and margarine; then add all remaining ingredients except shrimp. Divide shrimp between 2 large shallow baking pans; then pour 1/2 the heated sauce over each. Stir well, and cook in preheated oven for 15 to 20 minutes; turn shrimp in sauce once. Shells should be pink; do not overcook!

If it got any better than this recipe, it would be sinful! Thanks, Jo, for a truly outstanding shrimp treat.

Louisiana Creole Fillets

4-6 fresh thick white fish fillets	1/4 teaspoon garlic salt
1/4 teaspoon salt, plus extra	1/2 teaspoon Worcestershire sauce
1 (8-oz.) can tomato sauce	
2 oz. green pepper, finely chopped	3 drops Tabasco sauce
1 small onion, finely chopped	1 small bay leaf
1 small clove garlic, minced	

Soak fish fillets in salted water for 2 to 24 hours. Mix all remaining ingredients in a microwave-safe dish; cover and microwave on high for 2 minutes. Prepare a 2-or 3-quart shallow baking dish with spray-oil. Sprinkle salt on both sides of fillets; then place in baking dish. Pour hot Creole sauce over fillets, and bake at 350 degrees for 20 to 30 minutes depending on fillet thickness. After 20 minutes of baking, check fish for doneness. If fish is solid white, not transparent, and is flaky, it is done. Do not overcook.

Mozambique Lemoned Shrimp by Debbie

Make at least 4-1/2 hours in advance.

1-1/2 lbs. fresh jumbo shrimp
3 large cloves garlic, coarsely chopped
1 cup vegetable or peanut oil, divided

2 teaspoons crushed red pepper flakes
1 teaspoon salt
8 tablespoons unsalted butter, cut into slices
1/4 cup strained fresh lemon juice
Crusty hot French bread

Leaving the tail shells attached, carefully peel the shrimp, and devein. Wash the shrimp in 4 or 5 changes of fresh cold water, and drain. In a food processor or blender, pulverize the garlic, 1/2 cup of the oil, and the red pepper flakes. Pour the garlic mixture into a deep glass bowl, and stir in the remaining oil and salt. Add the shrimp, and gently mix to coat shrimp. Cover and refrigerate for 4 hours; stir occasionally. At cooking time, place shrimp on a grilling rack, and either grill or broil about 3-inches from heat for 2 to 3 minutes per side, or until shrimp are pink and firm; do not overcook. Arrange cooked shrimp on a heated serving platter, and cover to keep hot. In a small skillet, melt the butter until it foams; then immediately stir in the lemon juice. Pour the still foaming lemon mixture over the shrimp. Serve immediately with the crusty hot French bread. Serves 2 to 4.

Key West Snapper Fillets
by Joan

Salt and black pepper to taste	1 medium tomato, thinly sliced
2 lbs. fresh snapper or other fresh fish fillets	1 small green pepper, thinly sliced in rings
1/2 cup mayonnaise	2 tablespoons lemon juice
1 medium onion, thinly sliced in rings	Paprika
	3 tablespoons margarine

Preheat the oven to 350 degrees. Prepare a shallow 9- x 13-inch baking dish with spray-oil. Generously salt and pepper both sides of fillets, and place in the pan. Spread the mayonnaise on the tops of all the fillets. Layer each fillet with slices of onion, tomato, and green pepper in an attractive design. Sprinkle fillets with lemon juice and paprika; dot with margarine. Bake in the preheated oven for 20 to 30 minutes or until fish flakes easily and is a white color.

The presentation of this snapper recipe is most appealing, and the flavor tantalizing. Serve the fillets on a large elegant platter. Joan Backes, you've done it again!

Fresh Bass With Spicy Mushroom Sauce

Thick white fish fillets, other than bass, may also be used.

Salt and pepper to taste	4 oz. fresh or canned sliced
1 whole bass or bass fillets	mushrooms
2 tablespoons water	1/2 cup Worcestershire sauce
1 tablespoon lemon juice	1/8 teaspoon ground red pepper
4 oz. margarine	1 tablespoon minced chives

Prepare a 9- x 13-inch baking dish with spray-oil. Salt and pepper both sides of the bass; place in the baking dish. Add the water and the lemon juice. Bake bass at 350 degrees for 20 to 25 minutes or until done. Fish is done when it flakes easily and turns a white color. While fish is baking, melt the margarine in a small saucepan, and stir in the remaining ingredients. Heat and stir until sauce is hot. Pour the hot sauce over the cooked bass, and serve immediately. Serves 4.

Tuna Muffins

2 cups cooked, salted squash,	1 (12-oz.) can water-packed
mashed	tuna, drained
2 eggs	1/2 teaspoon freshly ground
1/2 cup self-rising corn meal	black pepper
1/2 cup plain flour	3/4 teaspoon salt
4 green onions, chopped with tops	1/4 teaspoon garlic powder
	1/4 teaspoon garlic salt

Prepare a 12-cup muffin pan with spray-oil. In a large bowl, combine all ingredients, and mix well. Fill the muffin cups, dividing mixture evenly. Bake at 350 degrees for 30 minutes or until muffins are set and test done.

The Fish Fry

    Ned Ellis tells the story of his family's unusual manner of celebrating the end of World War II. It was either V-E or V-J Day, no one seems to remember which, but everyone was beside themselves with jubilation. Ned's father, Hence, decided that a proper celebration for the whole town and surrounding area was in order. He directed the farmhands to break the dam on the fish pond near "The Big House." All the fish were caught with a seine as the water flowed out of the dam. That night Hence held a huge fish fry for the entire community.

    Now, if you should ever decide to fry an entire pond of fish, I just happen to have the recipe for you:

Deep-Fat Fried Fish
Yield: 300 servings, approximately 5 ounces each.

Fish Fillets................90 pounds	Eggs.......................................54
Salt..........................7-1/2 ounces	Milk..............................3 pints
Pepper........................3/4 ounce	Bread Crumbs............6 pounds

1. Cut fish into serving size pieces. 2. Dip fish in mixture of egg, milk, salt, and pepper. 3. Roll fish in bread crumbs. 4. Fry in deep fat, heated to 375 degrees F (a temperature at which a piece of day old bread will brown in 60 seconds) for 4 to 6 minutes or until brown. 5. Drain on absorbent paper 6. Serve immediately with a sauce.

    This recipe, very appropriately, came from an old Army cookbook, dated August 27, 1946. Dwight David Eisenhower was listed in the cookbook as Chief of Staff.

    Thanks to Helen and Grif Carden for loaning me this treasured old cookbook, from Grif's father's collection.

vegetables

Asparagus & Artichoke Casserole

2 (15-oz.) cans asparagus spears	1 cup sharp Cheddar cheese,
1 (14-oz.) can artichoke hearts	grated, plus extra
1 teaspoon seasoning salt	2 hard-boiled eggs, peeled
1/4 teaspoon ground black pepper	1 cup cracker crumbs
1 (10-3/4-oz.) can cream of	Paprika
celery soup	

Drain asparagus and artichokes; cut artichokes in quarters. Prepare a 9- x 13-inch baking dish with spray-oil. Make layers of asparagus and artichoke quarters; then sprinkle with seasoning salt and pepper. Continue layering with soup, cheese, eggs sliced thin, and cracker crumbs. Garnish with additional grated cheese, and sprinkle with paprika. Bake at 350 degrees for 40 minutes.

Our longtime friends Julia Mae and Leonard Gresham always bring this superb casserole to our Christmas-night dinner. Leonard is an accomplished pianist and is always gracious enough to provide us and our guests with a Christmas concert. He not only plays the piano, he GAVE us our beautiful piano. Julia Mae, his sister, grew up with my mother and aunt. She has a quality for quietly making you feel good and always "pitches in" when anyone needs help, including me! Julia Mae and Leonard have both tried to "wallpaper the Southeast" with my cookbooks as gifts to their friends. They should be due plenty of dinners in many homes!

Peppered Asparagus

1 lb. fresh, very tender asparagus	1 teaspoon soy sauce
1 cup water	1 teaspoon lemon juice
3/4 teaspoon salt	1/2 teaspoon fresh, coarsely
1 tablespoon margarine	ground black pepper

Trim tough ends from the asparagus; then wash. Cut asparagus in thin diagonal slices. Pour the water and salt in a medium saucepan. Place the asparagus in a steamer in the saucepan. Cover and cook for about 8 minutes until just tender. In a medium skillet, melt margarine; then add asparagus and the remaining ingredients. Toss the asparagus in the skillet over medium heat for about 2 minutes.

Bubber's Broccoli Bake

1 large head fresh broccoli	1 package Lipton's Onion
1 (8-1/2-oz.) can water chestnuts, drained	Soup Mix
1 cup pecan halves	1/2 cup margarine, melted

Wash broccoli, cut florets into quarters; then cut the stems in 1/4-inch diagonal slices. Place the florets and stem slices in unsalted boiling water, and bring to a boil again; then reduce heat to medium. Cover and cook 10 minutes; then drain. Place the cooked broccoli in a spray-oil prepared 2-quart baking dish. Slice the water chestnuts thin; then mix with the pecan halves and dry soup mix. Sprinkle over broccoli. Pour melted margarine over all ingredients, and gently toss. Cover and bake for 10 minutes. Serves 3 to 4.

This Bubber is my brother. He was nicknamed by me at a very early age. He's a super brother in more ways than I could ever tell and a very good chef. In fact, he's one of L.A.'s finest cooks, Lower Alabama that is. So when you are next in L.A. call Tommy Sparks and tell him that his sister invited you to dinner at his house! I may not survive this one???

Dutch Red Cabbage

1 medium head red cabbage,
   shredded
2 tablespoons margarine
3 tablespoons brown sugar
1/4 cup chopped onion
2 Granny Smith apples, peeled
   and diced

2 tablespoons vinegar
1/2 teaspoon salt
1/8 teaspoon coarsely ground
   black pepper
1/4 cup grape jelly or red
   plum jam

Saute the cabbage in the margarine for about 5 minutes, stirring often. Add the brown sugar, onion, and apples. Continue cooking for another 5 minutes. Add the remaining ingredients. Cover and simmer slowly for 20 minutes, stir occasionally. Serve hot. Serves 4 to 5.

Katrina's Garlic Green Beans

2 lbs. small fresh pole beans
1 cup water
3/4 teaspoon salt
1/4 cup margarine

4 large cloves garlic, minced
1/4 teaspoon lemon-pepper
   marinade

Wash pole beans, and remove the ends, pulling the strings. If needed, use a vegetable peeler to cut the sides to remove tough strings. Break beans into halves. In a Dutch oven, bring the water to a boil, and add salt and the beans. Return water to a boil; then cover and simmer for 10 minutes or until tender-crisp. Drain beans in a colander, and cover to keep warm. Add the margarine to the Dutch oven to melt; then add garlic, and cook slowly until garlic is tender. Stir in the lemon-pepper marinade and the cooked green beans. Cook, uncovered, for an additional 3 minutes. Spoon beans into a warm serving dish. Serves 4 to 8.

Mama's Green Tomato Bake

5 large green tomatoes, unpeeled and sliced thin	2 cups grated sharp Cheddar cheese
Salt	Ritz crackers, crumbled
1/2 cup margarine, sliced	Paprika

Prepare a 9- x 13-inch casserole with spray-oil. Make a layer of 1/2 tomatoes; then salt tomatoes. Place 1/2 the margarine slices on tomatoes; sprinkle with 1/2 the cheese and 1/2 the cracker crumbs. Repeat layers. Sprinkle with paprika. Cover casserole with aluminum foil, and bake at 350 degrees for 45 minutes; uncover and bake an additional 10 minutes.

You won't believe how good this tastes! And it is super easy. My Mama Does Know How To Cook!

Marjo's Cabbage Casserole

1/2 large head green cabbage, finely shredded	1 (10-3/4-oz.) can cream of celery soup
2 cups slightly crushed cornflakes, divided	1 cup milk
1/4 cup margarine, melted	1 cup grated sharp Cheddar cheese
1/2 cup Hellmann's mayonnaise	

Soak shredded cabbage in ice water for 30 minutes; then drain. In a large bowl, mix cornflakes with melted margarine. Prepare a 9- x 13-inch baking dish with spray-oil. Spread 1/2 of cornflake mixture on bottom of baking dish; then cover with drained cabbage. In a medium saucepan, combine mayonnaise, cream of celery soup, and milk; heat to just below boiling. Pour hot milk mixture over cabbage; then top with grated cheese and remaining cornflake mixture. Bake, uncovered, at 350 degrees for 30 to 45 minutes or until bubbling and lightly browned.

Marjo and John Gresham always have great, new recipes to try. They are both grand cooks and their delicious creations, along with their good senses of humor, are special assets.

Leonard's Marinated Slaw

Make 1 day in advance.	2 cucumbers, peeled and sliced thin
	1 large green pepper, cut in thin strips
4 cups very thinly shredded green cabbage	1 large onion, sliced in thin rings then chopped
2 carrots, scraped and sliced thin	

Marinade:	1 tablespoon salt
	1/2 cup sugar
2/3 cup white vinegar	1/2 teaspoon freshly ground black pepper
1/2 cup vegetable oil	2 cloves garlic, finely minced
1/4 cup water	

Prepare all vegetables, and place in a large bowl. In a small bowl, beat all of the marinade ingredients until very well mixed; then immediately pour over the vegetables. Toss to coat all the vegetables with the marinade. Cover and allow to stand at room temperature for 4 hours. The volume of the slaw will have decreased as the marinade wilts the vegetables. Taste for salt, and add, if needed. Place slaw in a glass or plastic bowl with a tight-fitting cover, and refrigerate. Slaw is ready to serve the next day. It will keep, refrigerated, for 7 days; give it a stir every day.

Mississippi Makin's

1 large onion, chopped	1/2 cup vegetable oil
1 lb. hot, bulk, light sausage	1/4 cup chopped green pepper
1 cup plain corn meal	1/4 cup chopped sweet red pepper
1/2 cup plain flour	1/2 cup cream-style corn
1 teaspoon salt	10 oz. grated sharp Cheddar
1/2 teaspoon baking soda	cheese
2 eggs, beaten	1 (16-oz.) can black-eyed peas,
1 cup buttermilk	rinsed and drained

In a large skillet, cook the onions and sausage while crumbling the sausage. Drain and discard the sausage drippings. In a large bowl, combine corn meal, flour, salt, and soda. In another large bowl, beat the eggs with the buttermilk and oil; then pour the buttermilk mixture in the corn meal mixture until barely blended. Stir in the remaining ingredients; then add the sausage mixture to blend. Prepare a 9- x 13-inch baking dish with spray-oil, and spread the mixture in the baking dish. Bake, uncovered, for 50 to 60 minutes until lightly browned. Allow to cool slightly before cutting in dinner-size squares.

Nippy Swiss Vegetable Bake

1 (16-oz.) package frozen broccoli, carrots, and cauliflower	1 (10-3/4-oz.) can cream of mushroom soup
4 oz. grated Swiss cheese	1/4 teaspoon coarsely ground black pepper
8 oz. Mexican Velveeta, cubed	1 (2.8-oz.) can French fried onion rings
1/3 cup sour cream	
4 oz. chopped pimentos, drained	

Thaw the vegetables, and drain; then mix all other ingredients except the onion rings with the vegetables. Prepare a shallow 2-quart baking dish with spray-oil; then pour in the vegetable mixture. Top with the onion rings. Bake at 350 degrees for 30 to 40 minutes. Serves 4 to 8.

Alfredo Sauce With Angel Hair Pasta

1/4 cup margarine
1 large clove garlic, minced
1/2 cup Half and Half
3/4 cup grated Parmesan cheese
4 drops Tabasco sauce

2 tablespoons finely chopped
   parsley (optional)
8-oz. angel hair pasta
Salt to taste
Coarsely ground black pepper
   to taste

In a Dutch oven, fill 1/2 full of salted water, and begin to boil. While water is coming to a boil, begin Alfredo sauce. In a skillet, using low to medium heat, melt margarine; then lightly cook garlic until soft. Stir in Half and Half, cheese, and Tabasco. Stir constantly until cheese melts and mixture thickens. Stir in parsley; set aside. After sauce is made and water is boiling, cook the angel hair pasta until just barely tender, about 3 minutes. Do not overcook; this pasta cooks very quickly. Just as soon as pasta is tender, pour into a colander to drain; do not rinse. Immediately pour hot pasta into hot Alfredo sauce, and very gently toss to blend, while heating on low. Salt and pepper to taste. Serves 4.

Calico English Peas

1 (16-oz.) package frozen small
   green peas
2 slices bacon
1/2 cup green onions sliced
   with tops

1/4 sweet red pepper, finely diced
Garlic salt to taste
2 drops Tabasco sauce

Place frozen peas in a colander, and rinse with cold water to defrost; allow to drain. In a skillet, cook bacon until crisp. Remove bacon to paper towel to drain. Add green onions to bacon drippings, and saute until lightly tender. Add sweet red pepper, cook 1 minute; then add drained peas. Cook until peas become thoroughly heated. Sprinkle with garlic salt to taste, and add Tabasco; toss and heat. Top with crumbled bacon. Serves 4 to 6.

Pecan Parmesan Noodle Casserole

1 (8-oz.) package medium-size egg noodles	3 cloves garlic, minced
1-1/2 teaspoons salt	6 saltine crackers, crushed
1/2 cup margarine, plus extra to toss noodles after cooking	Salt and pepper to taste
1 cup pecans, chopped	Grated Parmesan cheese
3/4 cup chopped fresh parsley	1 cup Half and Half
	Paprika to sprinkle

In a Dutch oven, cook the noodles with the 1-1/2 teaspoons of salt in lots of boiling water until just tender; do not overcook! Drain noodles as soon as they are tender, and toss with a small amount of extra margarine. While noodles are cooking, melt the 1/2 cup margarine, and saute the pecans, parsley, garlic, and crackers for about 5 minutes. Prepare a 2-quart baking dish with spray-oil. Make three layers of ingredients, beginning with 1/3 of the drained noodles, 1/3 pecan mixture, salt and pepper to taste; sprinkle liberally with grated Parmesan cheese. Repeat the layers 2 more times. Pour the Half and Half over the entire casserole; then run a flat-blade knife around the edges of the dish to allow the Half and Half to seep down. Cover and bake at 350 degrees for 35 minutes. Uncover and sprinkle with paprika; then cook an additional 5 minutes, or until just browned on top. Serves 6.

Colors of Italy Pasta

Pasta sauce:	2 teaspoons oregano
2 tablespoons olive oil	2 teaspoons chopped parsley
1 cup chopped onion	3/4 teaspoon sugar
3 large cloves garlic, crushed	1/4 teaspoon coarsely ground
2 (16-oz.) cans tomatoes, mashed	black pepper
to small pieces	Dash crushed red pepper flakes
2 teaspoons dried basil	Salt to taste

Pasta base:	1 cup part-skim ricotta cheese or
1/2 lb. washed fresh chopped	low-fat cottage cheese
spinach (frozen may be used)	1/4 cup skim milk
2 tablespoons olive oil	8 oz. vermicelli
1/2 teaspoon salt	Pasta sauce
1/4 teaspoon coarsely ground	1/2 cup grated Parmesan cheese
black pepper	

Pasta sauce: Pour olive oil in a saucepan, and saute the onion and garlic until tender. Add tomatoes, including the juice, and the remaining pasta sauce ingredients. Bring to a boil; then immediately reduce heat to simmer. Salt to taste. Simmer, uncovered, for about 30 minutes. Stir occasionally to blend, and break up tomato pieces to make into a sauce. Keep sauce warm.

Pasta base: In a large skillet, cook spinach and olive oil over medium heat about 10 minutes; stir constantly. Add salt, pepper, ricotta cheese, and skim milk. Cook over low heat until mixture is heated through; do not allow to boil. Cook vermicelli according to package directions, and drain. Do not overcook! On a large platter with a lip, top well-drained vermicelli with spinach sauce; then ladle pasta sauce over spinach. Sprinkle with grated Parmesan cheese. Makes 4 servings.

The colors in this dish are the colors in the flag of Italy. It is light, filling, and a great "no-meat" entree. Of course, if you just insist, you could add some cooked Italian sausage slices.

Italian Shells

1 lb. frozen spinach, thawed	1-1/2 teaspoons Dijon-style mustard
1 large clove garlic, minced	2 tablespoons grated Parmesan cheese
1 cup chopped onion	
1 large tomato, chopped	1 egg white, beaten
1/2 teaspoon garlic salt	1/2 lb. jumbo pasta shells, for stuffing
1/2 teaspoon salt	

Sauce :	1/2 teaspoon salt
1 (16-oz.) can tomatoes, chopped	1 teaspoon basil
1 clove garlic, minced	4 drops Tabasco sauce

In a skillet sprayed with oil, stir and cook the spinach, garlic, onion, and tomato until very wilted and blended. Add garlic salt, salt, mustard, and cheese; stir to blend. Add the beaten egg white, and blend thoroughly. Cook the pasta shells in salted water according to package directions; do not overcook. As soon as shells are tender, drain completely. Prepare a 9- x 13-inch baking pan with oil. Fill the shells with the spinach mixture and place in the pan.

Sauce: In a skillet, blend all ingredients, and simmer for 15 to 20 minutes. Spoon sauce over the tops of the filled pasta shells. Bake at 350 degrees for 30 minutes. Serves 4 to 6.

Sauteed Squash by John

2 lbs. small yellow squash	1 teaspoon salt
2 medium-size Vidalia onions	1 teaspoon fresh, coarsely ground black pepper, or more
2 tablespoons margarine	

Slice the squash thin, and the onions in very thin rings. In a large skillet, melt the margarine; and add the squash and onions. Sprinkle with the salt and pepper. Cook, uncovered, over medium heat until very soft. Add a small amount of water, only if needed.

Uncle Ed's New Year's Black-eyed Pea Soup

1 small hog jowl, or ham hock
Water for jowl or hock
3 (16-oz.) cans Bush's Best
  black-eyed peas, drained
1 medium yellow onion, chopped
1 medium green pepper, chopped
1 cup chopped celery
1 lb. smoked pork or turkey
  sausage, cubed
1 whole bay leaf
3 cups water
4 tablespoons catsup

1 tablespoon Worcestershire
  sauce
1/4 teaspoon ground black pepper
1/4 teaspoon Tabasco sauce
1/4 teaspoon Dale's Steak Sauce,
  if available
1/2 teaspoon Cavender's All
  Purpose Greek Seasoning
1 cup chopped fresh parsley
1 cup chopped green onions
  with tops

In a large Dutch oven, cover the hog jowl or ham hock with water. Bring
water to a boil for 2 minutes; then drain off the water. Add to the Dutch
oven with partially cooked hog jowl, the drained peas, yellow onion, green
pepper, celery, sausage, bay leaf, and the 3 cups of water. Additional water
may be needed. Bring to a boil, reduce heat to simmer, and cook,
uncovered, for 30 minutes. Stir occasionally. While the peas are
simmering, use a small bowl to combine the catsup, Worcestershire sauce,
black pepper, Tabasco, Dale's Steak Sauce, and Cavender's Greek
Seasoning. Mix to blend. When the 30-minute cooking time is completed,
stir in the spices combined in the small bowl. Continue simmering,
uncovered, and stirring for an additional 30 minutes; then stir in the parsley
and green onions. Remove the bay leaf; cook an additional 5 minutes, and
remove from heat. Serve hot with corn bread.

*Good luck for another year comes with this delicious soup. It is also
outstanding made without the extra seasonings combined in the small bowl.
Just stop the recipe short of those ingredients. Try the recipe made both
ways.*

Mike's Black Beans

1 (15-oz.) can Garcia's black beans
1 (10-oz.) can Ro-Tel tomatoes and green chilies
1 sliced green onion with top (optional)
Hot white rice (optional)

Drain the black beans in a colander; then place in a microwave-safe dish. Drain the Ro-Tel in the colander; mix the drained Ro-Tel with the drained black beans. Top with green onion slices. This may be served in several ways: hot over hot white rice, cold over hot white rice, hot or cold without rice.

Mike Mikell, our local pharmacist, is very health conscious. Often he will microwave this dish for lunch at the pharmacy. He's a busy man trying to help keep our small community healthy and well educated. But, with Mike, the old saying is so true, "If you really need something done, ask a busy man!" We probably ask too much, but he always comes through, even with good recipes. Thanks, Mike.

Caribbean Beans and Rice

1 large onion, diced
1 sweet red pepper, diced
3 large cloves garlic, minced
2 tablespoons olive oil
2 teaspoons ground ginger
1/4 teaspoon Tabasco sauce
1/2 teaspoon ground cumin
2 (15-oz.) cans black beans
2 tablespoons red wine vinegar
3/4 teaspoon salt
Hot white rice

In a Dutch oven, saute the onion, red pepper, and garlic in the olive oil until tender. Add ginger, Tabasco, cumin, and black beans; bring to a boil. Reduce heat, and simmer for 15 minutes. Add vinegar and salt; simmer for another 5 minutes. Serve over hot white rice. Serves 6.

Quick, Spicy Refried Beans

This is a microwave recipe. It can be served as a side dish, as the bottom layer for tacos, or as a dip with tortilla chips.

1 (28-oz.) can refried beans
Your favorite salsa to taste
1 cup grated sharp Cheddar
   cheese
Sliced jalapeno peppers (optional)

Reduced fat version :

1 (28-oz.) can no-fat refried beans
Your favorite salsa to taste

1 cup or less low-fat grated sharp
   Cheddar cheese
Sliced jalapeno peppers (optional)

Using a microwave-safe dish, combine all ingredients except the jalapeno peppers. Stir to blend; then microwave on high for 2 minutes. Stir and continue to microwave one minute at a time between stirrings until well blended and hot. Decorate the top with jalapeno peppers.

The jalapeno peppers may be removed by the faint of heart, mouth, stomach, etc., or they may be added by fire-eaters like me. Actually a small amount will satisfy my Mexican taste buds.

Spinach Croquettes

3 (10-oz.) packages frozen
   chopped spinach
2/3 cup finely diced cooked ham
6 oz. mozzarella cheese, grated

Salt and pepper to taste
2 eggs, divided
Italian bread crumbs
Vegetable oil

Cook spinach by package directions in salted water. Drain and press dry. In a large bowl, stir together the well-drained spinach, ham, and cheese until mixed; salt and pepper to taste. Beat 1 of the eggs; then stir into in the spinach mixture. Form this mixture into croquettes. In a small bowl, beat the remaining egg; then dip the croquettes in egg, and roll in crumbs. Fry croquettes in oil, and drain on paper towel. Serves 4.

Elegant Potato Torte

Paprika
9 medium-size Idaho potatoes
1 cup Swiss cheese, grated
1-1/2 to 2 cups Cheddar
   cheese, grated
4 tablespoons margarine, keep
   very firm

4 green onions chopped with tops
2 teaspoons salt
1/4 teaspoon coarsely ground
   black pepper
Fresh parsley sprigs or
   chopped parsley

Preheat the oven to 400 degrees. Prepare a deep 2-to 3-quart casserole, either round or square shape, with spray-oil, and sprinkle with paprika. Peel the potatoes, and place in a bowl; cover with cold water to prevent potatoes from turning dark. Mix the cheeses together; place on waxed paper or in a bowl. Dice (as best you can!) the firm margarine on another piece of waxed paper. Slice the green onions in rings including the tops, and place beside the margarine. In a small bowl, mix the salt and pepper. After these preparations are complete, slice the potatoes as thin as possible. Begin making the torte layers by placing a thin layer of sliced potatoes in the casserole; sprinkle with a small amount of the salt mixture, a small amount of the cheese mixture, a few onion slices, and a few margarine "dots." Repeat layers, keeping layers thin, until all ingredients are used. Cover the casserole, and bake in the preheated oven 1 and 1/2 hours or until potatoes are tender when pierced with a fork. Remove casserole from oven, and allow to cool 15 minutes. Run a knife around edges of casserole to loosen potatoes or cheese stuck to the dish. Using a serving platter, larger than the casserole, invert platter firmly over top of casserole; then invert both casserole and platter to turn torte onto the platter. Lift off the casserole. Place parsley sprigs on top of torte, or sprinkle with parsley. Serves 12.

This makes a spectacular presentation for the lowly pomme de terre!

Diane's Creamed Irish Potato Casserole

Make 1 day in advance, if possible.

8 to 10 medium-size Irish or
    Idaho potatoes
8 oz. cream cheese, softened
8 oz. sour cream

1/2 cup margarine, melted
1/4 cup chopped chives
1 clove garlic, minced
2 teaspoons salt
Paprika

Cook and peel the potatoes; then cut into chunks. In electric mixer, beat the cream cheese and sour cream; then add potatoes, a few chunks at a time, along with the melted margarine. Continue creaming the potatoes, and add the remaining ingredients except the paprika. Cream until very smooth. Prepare a 2-quart baking dish with spray-oil; then spoon the potato mixture into the dish. Sprinkle the top with paprika. Cover the dish, and refrigerate overnight. Remove from refrigerator about 15 minutes before baking. Bake, uncovered, at 350 degrees for 30 minutes, or until completely heated.

Red Garlic Potatoes

5 oz. small red or new potatoes,
    unpeeled
2 cloves garlic, peeled and halved
1/2 teaspoon salt
1 tablespoon margarine, softened

2 teaspoons finely chopped green
    onions or chives
1/2 medium sweet red pepper,
    chopped fine
Additional salt to taste

Wash potatoes, and split lengthwise. Place potatoes, garlic, and salt in saucepan; then add enough water to cover potatoes. Bring to a boil; place a loose piece of aluminum foil on top of pan, and reduce heat to a gentle boil. Cook about 10 minutes or until just tender. Do not cook to mush! Drain water, reserving potatoes and garlic. Remove garlic, and crush with a fork. Return potatoes and garlic to pan; add margarine, green onion, and red pepper. Toss over low heat to coat and heat. Add salt, if needed. Serves 2.

Judkins Squash Bake

2 lbs. small yellow squash	4 oz. chopped pimento
1/2 cup crushed Ritz crackers	3/4 teaspoon salt
1 egg, beaten	1/2 teaspoon garlic salt
1/4 cup margarine, melted	1/4 teaspoon liquid hot sauce
1 (5-oz.) can Pet milk	1/2 teaspoon black pepper
1 small onion, chopped	

Cook squash until tender; drain and press out as much water as possible. In a large bowl, mash the squash; then add all remaining ingredients. Mix until well blended. Prepare a shallow 2-quart baking dish with spray-oil. Spread squash mixture in the baking dish, and bake, uncovered, at 350 degrees for 30 to 40 minutes until lightly browned and set. Serves 4 to 6.

Cynthia Judkins Godbold, my cousin, and I share the Judkins family surname, and are close in age and friendship. We also share a love of good food. She has provided many great recipes to me throughout the years.

Summer Squash Supreme

2 lbs. small yellow squash	1 cup grated sharp Cheddar
1 medium onion, finely chopped	cheese
1 cup mayonnaise	12 saltine crackers, crushed
3 eggs, well beaten	1 cup bread crumbs
1 teaspoon salt	Paprika to sprinkle on top
1 (1-oz.) package dry buttermilk	1/4 cup margarine, melted
salad dressing mix	

Cook and drain squash; then press out all water. Place squash in a large bowl, and mash. Add onion, mayonnaise, beaten eggs, salt, dry buttermilk dressing mix, cheese, and crushed crackers; mix well to blend. Prepare a 9- x 13-inch baking dish with spray-oil. Spread the squash mixture in the baking dish. Sprinkle top with the bread crumbs, and paprika; then drizzle the melted margarine over the top. Bake, uncovered, at 350 degrees for 30 to 45 minutes.

Cheesy Potato Casserole

3 tablespoons margarine or butter	2 cups peeled, cooked, salted red potatoes
1/2 cup chopped onion	1/4 cup grated sharp Cheddar cheese
1/2 cup chopped green pepper	Salt and pepper to taste
3 tablespoons plain flour	Paprika
1-1/2 cups milk	

In a large skillet, melt margarine, and saute the onion and green pepper until soft. Stir in the flour, and cook until smooth and bubbly. Slowly add the milk, stirring until smooth and thickened. Slice the cooked potatoes in thin, round slices; then gently stir in sliced potatoes and cheese. Avoid breaking up the potatoes while mixing. Taste for salt and pepper; and add if needed. Prepare an 8- x 8-inch baking dish with spray-oil. Spread the potato mixture in the baking dish, and sprinkle with paprika. Bake at 350 degrees for about 30 minutes or until bubbling and hot.

Almond Rice

2 (10-1/2-oz.) cans beef broth	1 tablespoon margarine
1 cup Uncle Ben's Converted Rice	1/4 cup dry white wine (optional)
	3 tablespoons chopped parsley
1/2 cup sliced almonds	3 teaspoons chopped chives

In a medium saucepan, bring the beef broth to a boil, and add rice. Allow mixture to come back to a boil; then cover and reduce heat to simmer. Cook for 20 minutes; then remove from heat immediately, and uncover. In a small skillet saute the almonds in the margarine until golden brown. Add almonds and the remaining ingredients to the rice. Heat, stir, and blend until hot.

An elegant, easy side dish for almost any meat entree.

Crunchy-Topped Sweet Potato Casserole

Potatoes taste best if baked rather than boiled.	2 eggs, well beaten
	1/3 cup milk, or Pet milk
	1 cup granulated sugar
3 full cups cooked, whipped sweet potatoes	1/2 Granny Smith apple, finely diced
1/2 cup margarine, melted	1/2 cup raisins
1 teaspoon vanilla	2 tablespoons bourbon (optional)

Topping:	1/2 cup plain flour
	1 cup pecans, chopped
1 cup light brown sugar	1/3 cup margarine, melted

In a large bowl, mix all casserole ingredients until very well blended. In a medium bowl, mix all topping ingredients. Prepare a 9- x 13-inch baking dish with spray-oil. Spread the sweet potato mixture in the dish; then sprinkle with the topping. Bake, uncovered, at 350 degrees for 25 minutes.

Pecan Wild Rice Pilaf

1 (6-oz.) box Uncle Ben's Long Grain & Wild Rice	2 green onions, sliced very thin with tops
1/4 cup pecans, chopped	2 teaspoons grated orange rind, colored rind only
1 (1-1/2-oz.) individual box raisins	2 teaspoons orange juice

Prepare the rice according to package directions. After 15 minutes of cooking time for the rice, stir in the remaining ingredients. Cook for about 10 minutes more or until rice is tender and liquid absorbed. Remove from heat, and uncover to stop the cooking process. Serve immediately. Serves 3 to 4.

Jane's Pecan Rice

3 (10-1/2-oz.) cans chicken broth	1/2 cup sweet red pepper, diced
1 cup raw regular rice	1 (10-oz.) package frozen small green peas, uncooked
3 tablespoons margarine	1 tablespoon orange juice
1/2 cup pecans, coarsely chopped	1 teaspoon cooking sherry
4 green onions, chopped with tops	1 teaspoon garlic salt
8 oz. sliced fresh mushrooms	

In a large saucepan, bring chicken broth to a boil; then stir in the rice. Cover and reduce heat to simmer; cook 20 minutes. In a medium skillet, melt margarine, and add the pecans. Stir and cook for 2 minutes; then add green onions, mushrooms, and red pepper. Saute for an additional 3 minutes. When rice has completed the cooking time, add the pecan mixture to the cooked rice along with the remaining ingredients. Gently stir to blend all ingredients. Serves 6.

An absolutely delightful and different rice side dish. Jane Quint, of Mobile Alabama, is a perfect hostess. Her recipes are always outstanding and unique. She has taught me wonderful entertaining tips. Thanks, Jane, you are always there, and enthusiastic when I call for help!

Corn Puff Casserole

1/2 cup margarine, barely melted	1/2 cup frozen chopped onion or sauteed fresh onion
1 cup sour cream (no-fat may be used)	1 (16-oz.) can whole kernel corn, drained
1 egg, beaten	1 (16-oz.) can cream-style corn
	1 (9-oz.) box corn muffin mix

Preheat oven to 375 degrees. In a bowl, mix margarine, sour cream, and egg until blended. Stir in onion, both cans of corn; and dry muffin mix. Pour in a spray-oil prepared 8- x 8-inch casserole dish. Bake for 45 minutes to 1 hour until puffed, lightly brown, and crispy on top.

Truly out of this world!

Puff Spinach Pinwheels

1 (10-oz.) package frozen chopped spinach	1/4 cup grated Parmesan cheese
1 sheet from a 17-1/4-oz. package frozen puff pastry, thawed	1 green onion, chopped with top
	1/8 teaspoon garlic powder
1 egg, well beaten	1/2 teaspoon salt
1 tablespoon water	1/4 teaspoon Tabasco sauce
2 oz. Monterey Jack cheese, grated	1/4 cup chopped pecans

Preheat oven to 400 degrees. Thaw spinach by running hot water over the spinach in a colander; then press with a fork to drain thoroughly. Place the opened sheet of the puffed pastry on a lightly floured board. Beat egg and water together; then brush one side of the pastry with the egg mixture, taking care to heavily coat all of the edges. In a bowl, combine the drained spinach and the remaining ingredients; mix very well. Spread the spinach mixture over the entire surface of the pastry. On the longest side of the pastry, begin to roll the pastry jelly roll style; place the ending edge down. If time permits, chill the roll in the refrigerator before slicing in 12 equal pinwheels. Place the pinwheels on a spray-oil prepared cookie sheet, and brush the tops with the remaining egg mixture. Bake in the preheated oven for 20 minutes or until golden and lightly browned. Makes 12.

Quite easy to make, yet appears to have taken days of preparation. My kind of recipe!

Becky's Ritzy Baked Spinach Supreme

2 (10-oz.) packages frozen
   chopped spinach
1 pint cottage cheese, divided
1 lb. medium Cheddar cheese,
   grated and divided
1 lb. mozzarella cheese, grated
   and divided

6 eggs
1/4 cup vegetable oil
1/2 lb. sharp Cheddar cheese,
   grated
1 roll of a 1 lb. box Ritz crackers

Cook spinach according to directions on the package with salt. Drain spinach in a colander, and press the spinach until dry. In a small bowl, combine 1/2 cup of the cottage cheese, 1/2 of the medium Cheddar cheese, and 1/2 cup of the mozzarella cheese. Mix to blend, and reserve for later. In a large bowl, beat the eggs very well; then add the drained spinach, oil, the remaining cottage cheese, medium Cheddar cheese, mozzarella cheese, and all of the sharp Cheddar cheese. Stir and mix all ingredients. Crush and stir in enough Ritz crackers to make the mixture a corn bread consistency. Prepare a shallow 9- x 13-inch baking dish with spray-oil; then spread the spinach mixture in the baking dish. Sprinkle the top with the reserved mixture of cheeses. Bake, uncovered at 400 degrees for 40 to 45 minutes, or until top is browned. Allow to cool 10 minutes before cutting. Serves 8 to 10.

This makes a large, very hearty vegetable casserole. Actually the spinach is a good excuse to hold together lots of cheese and eggs! Excellent dish.

Spinach Napoli

1 (10-oz.) package frozen
   chopped spinach
1 small clove garlic, minced
1 tablespoon olive oil
1/4 teaspoon salt
1/8 teaspoon coarsely ground
   black pepper
	2 tablespoons freshly grated
	   Parmesan cheese, divided
	1 large egg, well beaten
	1 slice bacon, fried, drained, and
	   crumbled (optional)

Cook spinach by package directions in salted water; drain and press dry. In a large skillet, saute garlic in olive oil over low heat until golden brown. Add spinach, salt, and pepper; mix until well blended. Spread mixture over the bottom of the skillet. Sprinkle with 1 tablespoon Parmesan cheese. Cook, turning frequently, until the mixture is well heated. Add egg, and continue to cook like scrambling eggs, until the egg is firm but not dry. Add bacon, and stir until well mixed. Turn mixture onto a serving platter, and sprinkle with the remaining Parmesan cheese. Serves 2.

Outstanding! You know that spinach alone needs a little help. . .this is the ticket to delicious help; leave it to the Italians.

Latin Style Green Beans

1 medium onion, chopped
1 teaspoon olive oil
1 (14-1/2-oz.) can Mexican stewed
   tomatoes
	1 (28-oz.) can cut green beans,
	   drained
	1/4 teaspoon salt
	1/4 teaspoon garlic salt
	Seasoned croutons

In a skillet, saute the onion in the olive oil. Add the tomatoes, and mash to break into small pieces. Add the drained green beans; sprinkle with the two salts. Stir then simmer for 15 minutes. Add the seasoned croutons just as the dish is served to keep them crunchy. Serves 4.

Greek Stuffed Eggplant

Select eggplant with no green color showing.

2 eggplants, 1/2 lb. each
Salt, divided
4 tablespoons olive oil, divided
1 cup chopped onion
2 large cloves garlic, minced

1/3 cup fresh minced parsley leaves
3 tablespoons minced fresh mint leaves
3 Roma tomatoes, diced
6 oz. crumbled feta cheese
1/2 teaspoon Cavender's Greek All Purpose Seasoning
Paprika to sprinkle on top

Cut eggplants in half lengthwise; then cut the pulp of 3 halves with a knife, leaving 1/2-inch-thick eggplant shells. Sprinkle shells with salt, and invert on paper towels for 30 minutes. Peel skin from remaining half eggplant; cut it, along with the scooped-out pulp of the other eggplant halves, in 1/2-inch pieces. Place pieces in a bowl of cold, salted water for 20 minutes; then drain in colander. Preheat broiler to 500 degrees. After shells have drained for the 30 minutes, pat dry with paper towel, and brush with 1 tablespoon of the olive oil. Broil shells about 4-inches from heat for 5 minutes or until tender. After pulp has soaked and drained, pat dry with paper towel. In a large skillet, heat the remaining olive oil over medium-high heat until hot, but not smoking. Saute eggplant pulp until golden; then stir in onion and garlic. Cook until onion is softened. Remove skillet from heat, and stir in remaining ingredients; then salt to taste. Fill shells with eggplant mixture, sprinkle with paprika, and broil until bubbling hot and browned. Serves 3 to 6.

A perfect dish for the feta cheese aficionado. Irene and Marshall Logan, my cousins, have contributed this special Greek dish by way of Florida, which is their home. The Greek people are great eggplant lovers, and truly know how to prepare it in many wonderful ways. The selection of the eggplant, along with the salting and draining are the secrets to great eggplant dishes like this.

Hot Fruit Casserole

The canned fruit can be in natural juices or in heavy syrup.

1 (20-oz.) can pineapple chunks
1 (29-oz.) can peach halves
1 (29-oz.) can pear halves
2 (16-oz.) cans apricot halves
2 (11-oz.) cans mandarin oranges

1 (10-oz.) jar maraschino cherries
1/4 to 1/3 cup brown sugar
Cinnamon to sprinkle
1/4 cup dry sweet wine (optional)
1/3 cup cornstarch

Select the two favorite fruits; drain their juices in a bowl, and reserve. Drain all of the remaining fruits, and discard their liquid. Prepare a shallow 9- x 13-inch baking dish with spray-oil. Arrange the fruit in the bottom of the baking dish, and sprinkle with the brown sugar and a small amount of cinnamon. Bake, uncovered, at 350 degrees for 30 to 40 minutes. Remove baking dish from oven. In a small bowl, stir 3/4 cup of the reserved fruit juice and the wine into the cornstarch until mixture is smooth. (May use 1 cup of reserved fruit juice without the wine.) Pour the cornstarch mixture over the fruit, and return the baking dish to the oven to bake an additional 10 minutes or until fruit is glazed.

Fulghom's Favorite Baked Apricot Casserole

2 (16-oz.) cans light or regular apricots, drained
1/4 cup brown sugar

2 tablespoons margarine
12 to 15 Ritz or saltine crackers, crumbled

Prepare a 1-1/2-quart baking dish with spray-oil. Place the apricots rounded side down in the bottom of the dish. Sprinkle with the brown sugar, and dot with small pieces of the margarine. Top with the crumbled crackers. Bake at 350 degrees for 30 minutes. Serves 4.

Jay Payne's Green Bean Bacon Bundles

Marinate overnight, if possible.

1 (16-oz.) can whole green beans, rinsed and drained
3 bacon strips
1 tablespoon soy sauce
2 tablespoons Worcestershire sauce
3 tablespoons prepared Italian salad dressing

Garlic powder to sprinkle
Lemon-pepper marinade to sprinkle
1 tablespoon margarine
4 oz. slivered almonds
4 oz. whole pimentos, cut in long strips
3 to 4 oz. black olives, sliced (optional)

Cut bacon slices in half while bacon is cold; then separate the halves to allow bacon to come to room temperature. Carefully divide the whole green beans into bundles of 10 to 12 green beans each. Stretch and wrap twice, if possible, each bacon half around center of each green bean bundle. Secure bacon with a toothpick. Prepare a shallow 1-1/2-quart baking dish with spray-oil; then place bundles in the baking dish. In a small bowl, combine soy sauce, Worcestershire sauce, and Italian salad dressing; pour over the bundles. Sprinkle bundles with a very small amount of garlic powder and a light sprinkle of lemon-pepper marinade. Cover and marinate in refrigerator overnight, if possible. Bundles will still be good if not marinated. At cooking time, uncover; and bake at 400 degrees for about 25 minutes or until bacon is browned and crisp. Baste once or twice during cooking time. While bundles are cooking, melt margarine in a small skillet, and lightly brown almonds. When almonds are browned, add pimento strips and black olive slices, and gently saute until warm. Remove cooked bundles to a warm platter with a slotted spoon, and garnish with the almond mixture.

James Dixon Payne, or "Jay" as we know him, makes this perfectly wonderful green bean dish. The appearance is particularly appealing, and the flavors are superb. He has exquisite taste both in foods and in antiques. It is always a treat to the eye, and the palate, when he entertains.

caramelized Spanish onions

3 very large Idaho-Oregon onions	2 teaspoons thyme
1/4 cup margarine	1/2 teaspoon salt
1/4 cup granulated sugar	1/8 teaspoon fresh, coarsely
3 teaspoons brown sugar	ground black pepper

Peel and slice onions in 1-inch slices. Place onion slices in a microwave-safe dish, and cover. Microwave on high for 5 minutes. In a large skillet, melt the margarine, and add the onion slices. Coat the whole onion slices with margarine, being careful not to separate the rings. In a small bowl, combine both sugars, thyme, salt, and pepper. Sprinkle one teaspoon of the spice mixture evenly over each onion slice. Heat the skillet to medium high. Using a spatula, turn the onion slices, spice side down, to cook for 5 minutes. Sprinkle the other side with the spices, and turn to cook that side for 5 minutes. Turn again to cook 1 minute longer on each side. Add additional salt, if needed.

windy Hill Potato casserole

4 large Idaho potatoes, cooked and peeled	1 cup chopped onion
Salt and pepper	4 oz. chopped pimentos
1 cup grated sharp Cheddar cheese	1 (4-oz.) can chopped green chilies
	1 (10-3/4-oz.) can cream of chicken soup

Use a 3-quart shallow baking dish prepared with spray-oil. Slice the cooked potatoes to cover the bottom of the dish; salt and pepper to taste. In a bowl, mix all remaining ingredients, and spread over the potatoes. Bake at 350 degrees for 45 minutes. Serves 6 to 8.

Eggs & Cheese

Dixie Breakfast Casserole

Grits:	1/2 cup quick grits
	1/2 teaspoon salt (no substitutes)
2 cups water	Milk

Casserole:	1 (6-oz.) package corn bread mix
	Salt and pepper to taste
1 lb. bulk sausage, hot or mild	4 eggs, well beaten
1-3/4 cups hot milk	1 cup grated sharp
1/2 cup margarine, melted	Cheddar cheese

Grits: In a Dutch oven, bring water to a boil. Slowly stir in grits and salt. Cook grits, uncovered, until they begin to pop out of pot. Remove pot from heat, and stir in a small amount of milk to make mixture slightly "soupy." Immediately return pot to heat, and cover. Reduce heat to simmer, and cook until grits have thickened. When grits have thickened, remove pot from heat, and set aside. While grits are cooking, begin casserole.

Casserole: Cook and crumble sausage; drain well. In a large bowl, mix 2 cups of hot cooked grits with the hot milk, melted margarine, and dry corn bread mix. Taste for salt and pepper; add if needed. Stir in eggs until very well mixed. Prepare a 9- x 13-inch baking dish with spray-oil. Spread cooked and drained sausage on bottom of dish. Pour grits mixture over sausage. Sprinkle top of the casserole with cheese, and bake at 325 degrees for 45 minutes. Allow to cool for 5 minutes before cutting in squares.

As my mother would say, " super deelaah!"

Kentucky Egg Casserole

May be prepared 1 or 2 days in advance and refrigerated before baking.

1/2 cup chopped onions
4 tablespoons margarine
4 tablespoons plain flour
2-1/2 cups milk

2 cups grated, sharp Cheddar cheese
12 hard-boiled eggs, peeled and sliced
1-1/2 cups crushed potato chips
20 slices bacon, cooked and crumbled

In a large skillet, saute the onions in the margarine. Stir in the flour; then gradually stir in the milk, keeping the mixture smooth. Stirring constantly, cook over medium heat until mixture is thickened. Stir in cheese, and continue to heat and stir until cheese is melted. Prepare a shallow 9- x 13-inch casserole dish with spray-oil. Cover the bottom of the casserole with all of the egg slices; then spread the cheese sauce over the eggs. Sprinkle potato chips over the sauce; then top with the crumbled bacon. Bake at 350 degrees for 30 minutes. Serves 8 to 12.

This recipe comes from David Rennekamp, who declares that every elegant Kentucky hostess serves this before setting off with her guests on the day of the Kentucky Derby. Tastes good for any special morning occasion.

Shrimp & Crab Tart

No extra salt is needed in the recipe.

1 lb. fresh small or medium-size shrimp
3 tablespoons margarine, divided
Prepared Italian salad dressing
1 (9-inch) folded commercial refrigerator pie crust, unbaked
1/4 cup chopped green onions, with tops
1/4 cup celery, chopped

1/4 cup chopped sweet red pepper
2 to 3 oz. fresh small mushrooms, sliced
1 large egg, beaten
1/4 cup mayonnaise
1 tablespoon lemon juice
1/4 teaspoon Tabasco sauce
1/4 cup grated Parmesan cheese
6 to 7 oz. fresh crabmeat or canned crabmeat, drained
1-1/3 cups grated sharp Cheddar cheese, divided

Peel and wash shrimp in 5 changes of fresh, cold water; then drain. Do not cheat! In a large skillet, melt 1 tablespoon of the margarine, and saute the shrimp for only a short time. As soon as shrimp turn pink, remove skillet from heat. Do not overcook; since the shrimp will cook again in the tart. Preheat oven to 400 degrees. In a medium bowl, marinate 1/2 of the shrimp in just enough Italian salad dressing to cover the shrimp while the remaining recipe is being prepared; set aside. Place pie crust in a 9-inch round baking dish. Crimp edges of crust to form a lip. Prick pie crust with a salad fork, and bake in the preheated oven for 5 to 7 minutes. Set aside pie crust to completely cool. In medium skillet, melt the remaining margarine. Saute green onion, celery, red pepper, and mushrooms until soft. In a large bowl, vigorously beat egg with mayonnaise, lemon juice, Tabasco sauce, Parmesan cheese, and crabmeat. Add 1 cup of the Cheddar cheese, the unmarinated shrimp, and the mushroom mixture; mix to blend. Using a slotted spoon, add the marinated shrimp; discard marinade. Pour tart mixture in cooled pie crust, and bake at 350 degrees for 20 minutes. Sprinkle the remaining Cheddar cheese over tart, and bake an additional 10 minutes. Serves 4 to 8.

Baked Deviled Eggs
by Nancy

6 eggs	3 tablespoons sour cream
2 teaspoons prepared mustard	1/4 teaspoon salt

Sauce:

2 tablespoons margarine	3/4 cup sour cream
1/2 cup finely chopped green pepper	1/2 cup grated sharp Cheddar cheese
1 (10-3/4-oz.) can cream of mushroom soup	1/4 cup chopped pimento
	Paprika

Hard boil the eggs; peel and cut in half lengthwise. Scoop the yolks out of the white shells into a bowl. Mash the yolks with a fork until finely crumbled; then mix in the mustard, 3 tablespoons sour cream, and salt until well blended. Fill the egg whites with the egg yolk stuffing; set aside. To make the sauce, melt the margarine and saute the green pepper until limp; then stir in the remaining ingredients except paprika. Cook for 2 minutes. Prepare a shallow 8- x 8-inch baking dish with spray-oil; pour 1/2 of the sauce into the baking dish. Place stuffed eggs in the dish on top of sauce. Pour the remaining sauce over the eggs, and sprinkle with paprika. Bake at 350 degrees for 30 minutes or until heated throughout. Serves 6 to 8.

Dutch Baby

1/2 cup butter	Powdered sugar
6 eggs	Fresh sliced fruit of choice
1-1/2 cups plain flour	(optional)
1-1/2 cups milk	

Place the butter in a large iron skillet in the oven at 425 degrees. In a food processor or blender, mix the eggs until well blended; then add the flour and milk. Blend until smooth. When butter is completely melted and skillet is hot remove the skillet from the oven. Carefully and slowly pour the egg mixture in the center of the hot melted butter to form a pool of egg mixture surrounded by butter. Return skillet to oven, and turn on oven light. Watch the "Baby" grow up through the glass door. Remove skillet from the oven when the "Baby" is 2-or 3-inches high and lightly browned on top. This will take approximately 15 to 20 minutes. Liberally sprinkle the top with sifted powdered sugar, and arrange the fruit on top, if desired. Cut in wedges, and serve immediately before the "Baby" cools and shrinks! Serves 4 to 8.

If you would prefer individual "Babies," use a very small skillet with 1-1/2 tablespoons butter, 1 egg, 1/4 cup plain flour, and 1/4 cup milk.

Our friend David Rennekamp has lived in Europe for a number of years and served on the faculty of the Air War College at Maxwell Air Force Base in Montgomery, Alabama. He was given this recipe, already titled, by the daughter of Dutch immigrants. A favorite of all of the Rennekamps.

Sour Cream Pancakes with Pecans

Make small silver dollar-size pancakes.

2-1/2 cups plain flour
1 tablespoon baking powder
1 tablespoon granulated sugar
2 teaspoons baking soda
1 teaspoon salt

3 eggs
2 cups buttermilk
1 cup sour cream
2 tablespoons margarine, melted
1/2 cup pecans, chopped
Vegetable oil for cooking

In a large bowl, sift the flour, baking powder, sugar, baking soda, and salt. In another large bowl beat eggs; then add buttermilk and sour cream until blended. Stir in the melted margarine and pecans. Beat in the flour mixture until well blended. Pour a small amount of vegetable oil in a heavy, large skillet; and heat to hot, but not smoking. Reduce heat to medium-hot; and pour off excess oil, leaving only a small film of oil in the skillet. Spoon batter on the skillet to make pancakes. Allow pancakes to lightly brown and set on 1 side before turning to cook the other side. When cooking the remaining batter, add only 2 or 3 drops of oil to the skillet for each cooking of the pancakes. Serve hot with blackberry or other fruit preserves, or syrup.

These are divine for breakfast or for Sunday-night supper.

German Apple Pancake

Makes 1 large pancake that is
served in wedges.

4 tablespoons margarine, divided
1/2 cup sugar
1/4 cup water
6 medium-size Granny Smith
    apples; peeled, cored, cut in
    very thin slices lengthwise

3 eggs
3/4 cup milk
3/4 cup plain flour
1/4 teaspoon salt
1/2 cup pecans, chopped

Preheat oven to 425 degrees. In a large iron skillet, melt 2 tablespoons of the margarine. Add sugar and water; then bring to boiling. Add apple slices and stir; then cook, covered, on medium for 15 minutes. Stir twice. While apples are cooking, beat all remaining ingredients, except the remaining margarine, in a large bowl, until smooth and well blended. When apples are cooked, spoon the apples into a colander placed over a bowl to reserve the juice; press lightly to extract juice. The juice will be very slight, and used as a light syrup later. Add the cooked apple slices to the egg mixture, and stir. Wash skillet, and dry completely. Add the remaining 2 tablespoons margarine to the skillet, and place in the preheated oven until margarine is melted and skillet is hot. Remove skillet from oven; then slowly and carefully pour the egg mixture in the center of the melted margarine in the hot skillet. Return skillet to the oven, and bake for 15 minutes at 425 degrees; then reduce heat to 400 degrees for 15 minutes. Remove skillet from oven. Heat the small amount of apple liquid, and pour over the pancake. Immediately remove the pancake to a platter, and serve hot. Serves 4 to 6.

Baked Green Chilies Cheese Grits

4 cups boiling water	1/8 teaspoon garlic salt
1 teaspoon salt (no substitutes)	1/4 teaspoon cayenne pepper
1 cup quick grits	1 (4.5-oz.) can chopped green
Milk	chilies, undrained
1/2 cup margarine	2 eggs, well beaten
12 oz. sharp Cheddar cheese, grated	

In a Dutch oven, bring the water and salt to a full boil. Stirring the water vigorously, slowly pour in the grits to keep from lumping. Bring grits back to a boil; then cook, uncovered, on high-heat until grits begin to thicken and pop out of the pot. Cover and lower heat to medium-low for 1 minute. Uncover and stir; then add enough milk to make the grits a little "soupy." Cover again, and simmer for about 5 to 10 minutes. After the initial cooking time is finished; add margarine, cheese, and enough milk to make the grits "soupy" again. Heat on low to allow cheese to melt; stir to blend. Add garlic salt, cayenne pepper, and undrained green chilies. Blend all ingredients then add the beaten eggs, and mix well. Prepare a shallow 9- x 13-inch baking dish with spray-oil, and pour in the grits mixture. Bake, uncovered, at 350 degrees for about 50 minutes. Remove from oven, and allow to cool for about 5 minutes before serving. Serves 6 to 8.

Scrambled Alaskan Salmon

4 slices bacon	3/4 teaspoon salt, divided
1 small onion, minced	8 eggs
2 cups frozen, shredded hash brown potatoes, thawed	1 cup grated sharp Cheddar cheese
1 (16-oz.) can salmon, drained and boned	4 drops Tabasco sauce

Fry bacon in a skillet; remove bacon to drain, and reserve drippings. Saute the onion, hash browns, and salmon in 4 tablespoons of the drippings until tender. Sprinkle with 1/2 teaspoon of the salt. Beat eggs; then stir in the cheese, Tabasco, and remaining 1/4 teaspoon salt. Pour the egg mixture in the hot hash brown mixture, and scramble. Crumble the crisp bacon on top. Serves 8.

Amsterdamer's Brunch

4 thick slices white bread, buttered and toasted	4 long, thin dill pickle slices; halved
8 slices cooked ham	4 over-light fried eggs, salted and peppered
4 lettuce leaves	
8 thin slices fresh tomato, salted	8 drops Tabasco sauce
4 teaspoons mayonnaise	Paprika

Place 2 slices of toast on 2 dinner plates. Make layers on each toast slice of 2 slices of meat, 1 lettuce leaf, 2 tomato slices, 1 teaspoon mayonnaise, 2 dill pickle halves, 1 fried egg, 2 drops Tabasco, and a sprinkle of paprika. Serve open face with a knife and fork. Serves 2 to 4.

Traveling Breakfast Sandwiches

This is a handy recipe if you are traveling early by automobile and do not want to stop for breakfast. Make the sandwiches the day before departure.	**1 English muffin or bagel per person** **Cheese of choice: sharp Cheddar or Velveeta** **Bulk sausage or sliced link sausage, cooked**

Split the English muffin or bagel, and place sliced cheese on one muffin half. Add sausage amount to suit yourself; then add more cheese slices. Place the plain muffin half on top. After making the desired number of sandwiches, wrap several sandwiches in heavy aluminum foil; and crimp the edges to seal tight. Place the foil packages in the refrigerator; then make a reminder note to place the packages in the oven upon arising. Place the note where it will be found first thing in the morning. The next morning, bake the packages at 350 degrees until sandwiches are toasted and cheese is melted. Keep packages tightly wrapped to keep warm until time to eat.

This is an easy, delicious, time-saving, and inexpensive recipe! Plus it does not get crumbs all over your automobile. It usually suits almost everyone's taste, even the "picky" ones. What more could you ask?

Stories from the Victorian Verandah

The Disappearance

Every year for the last 25 years, Fort Deposit has held an annual two-day spring festival, Calico Fort. It, of course, draws everyone from Fort Deposit and a huge crowd from the state as a whole. In the days before Priester's retail store was opened, the entire town closed and went to Calico Fort for two full days of festivities and helping with the various booths.

It had long been the habit of L. C. Priester, founder of Priester's Pecan Company, to check the massive, room-size pecan cooler for temperature consistency. He was a man highly concerned with the quality of his product.

On the opening Saturday morning of Calico Fort, L. C. dashed by the warehouse to check the temperature in the cooler. What happened next would make a great movie script. While L. C. was in the cooler, the electric power went off, leaving him in total darkness and hearing the heavy thud of the huge door closing! He was trapped.

His calls for help went unanswered, since everyone else was enjoying themselves at the festival.

He began to become concerned about lack of oxygen. Finding a vent, he stuck his nose in it to breathe, while hammering on the door and calling for help.

Mrs. Priester didn't find it at all unusual that she hadn't seen L. C. all day. They had been scheduled to be busy helping with the daylong events. But as late afternoon approached, she became concerned. They had planned to attend a wedding in Montgomery, and L. C. was nowhere to be found at the festival. She decided to check the warehouse, suspecting that he may have slipped off to do a little work.

As she entered the warehouse, she heard his faint cries for help and a hammering noise on the cooler wall. Quickly she called the emergency squad, who arrived to free L. C. and swaddled him in layers of blankets.

Mr. Priester really knew how to spend a fun Saturday!

P. S. In L. C.'s understandable panic, he had forgotten the manual door-release in the cooler designed for just such an emergency!

Breads

Ellen's Sour Cream Corn Bread

1 cup self-rising corn meal mix	3 eggs, well beaten
1 cup sour cream	1/2 cup vegetable oil
1 (8-3/4-oz.) can cream-style corn	

Preheat oven to 350 degrees. In a medium bowl, mix all of the ingredients until well blended. Prepare an 8- x 8-inch baking pan with spray-oil. Pour mixture in the pan, and bake in the preheated oven for 35 to 40 minutes or until lightly browned. Cut in squares to serve hot.

A favorite of Ellen Ellis Burkett, one of the family owners and managers of Priester's Pecan Company, plus a wife and mother. She never ceases to amaze me with all of her many skills, which she performs with quiet, lady-like efficiency. This recipe is outstanding for taste and on-the-go ease.

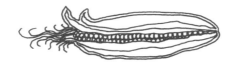

Marshall Green's Biscuits

4 heaping tablespoons Crisco shortening	1 cup buttermilk
2 cups self-rising flour	

Preheat oven to 450 degrees. In a medium bowl, cut the shortening into the flour until very well mixed and crumbly. Slowly stir in the buttermilk to form a soft dough. Roll out on a lightly floured board to 3/4-inch thickness, and cut with a small biscuit cutter. Place biscuits on a spray-oil prepared baking pan, and bake in the preheated oven for 12 minutes or until browned. Makes 12.

Marshall Green is an uncle of the Ellis family. His biscuits are divine. I have elaborated slightly on his instructions, since he seems to be a man of few words. Only one sentence of instruction! But then, who needs words when hot biscuits are coming out of the oven?

Great Cheese Biscuits

12 Marshall Green's biscuits (see recipe above)	12 medium-thick slices New York State Cheddar cheese

Follow the recipe for Marshall Green's biscuits. Just as soon as the biscuits are removed from the oven, split biscuits, and place a slice of cheese inside. Immediately return the cheese-stuffed biscuits to the oven; then turn oven off. Turn light on in the oven, and watch biscuits carefully until cheese begins to melt. It will only take a couple of minutes. Remove cheese biscuits from oven, and enjoy.

Hamilton's Jazzy Corn Bread

4 slices bacon	3 eggs, well beaten
1 cup self-rising corn meal mix, yellow (if available)	1/2 cup vegetable oil
1 cup sour cream	1-1/2 oz. pickled, mixed-variety salad pepper rings, hot or mild

Cook bacon until very crisp, and reserve 2 tablespoons bacon drippings. Crumble bacon, and set aside. Preheat oven to 350 degrees. Put reserved bacon drippings in a 8- x 8-inch or a 2-quart baking pan. Place the pan in the oven, and heat until hot. In a large bowl, mix the corn meal, sour cream, beaten eggs, and oil until well blended. Stir in the crumbled bacon and drained pepper rings. Pour 1 tablespoon of the hot drippings in the corn bread mixture, and beat to blend. Tilt the baking pan to coat the inside bottom and sides of the pan with the remaining bacon drippings. Pour mixture in pan, and bake in the preheated oven for 35 to 40 minutes or until lightly browned. Cut in squares to serve hot.

Orange Biscuits

2 cups plain flour	4 tablespoons margarine
2 tablespoons granulated sugar	1 teaspoon grated orange rind
2 teaspoons baking powder	1/3 cup milk
1/2 teaspoon salt	1/3 cup orange juice

Preheat oven to 375 degrees. Measure flour, and sift; then re-measure flour by spooning lightly into cup. Re-sift flour with sugar, baking powder, and salt. In a bowl, cut the margarine and orange rind into the flour mixture with a fork or pastry cutter until very well mixed. Gradually add the milk and the orange juice until a soft dough is formed. Roll out dough on a lightly floured board to a thickness that will allow 12 small, round biscuits to be cut from the dough. Prepare a pan with spray-oil, and place biscuits on the pan. Bake in the preheated oven for about 15 minutes or until lightly browned on bottom and top. Makes 12.

Quick Potato Biscuits

1/2 cup instant mashed potato flakes	1 cup very hot water
1 teaspoon granulated sugar	1/3 cup cold water
2 tablespoons margarine, very soft	3 cups biscuit mix

Preheat oven to 450 degrees. In a small bowl, mix the potato flakes and sugar. Add the margarine and hot water; mix well. Add cold water and biscuit mix. Work mixture to form a soft dough, using a small amount of additional cold water, if needed. Turn out on a lightly floured board, and knead 10 times. Roll out with a rolling pin to 1/2 to 3/4-inch thickness, and cut with a small floured biscuit cutter. Place biscuits on an ungreased baking pan, and bake in the preheated oven for 10 to 15 minutes or until lightly browned. Makes 25 small biscuits.

Deviled Rolls

3/4 cup plain flour	2 tablespoons ice water
1/8 teaspoon salt	1 (3-1/4-oz.) can deviled ham
1/4 cup vegetable shortening	

In a food processor with a steel blade, dry mix the flour and salt; then add the shortening and ice water to make a stiff dough. Roll out the dough with a floured rolling pin on a lightly floured board in an oblong shape. Spread the dough with the deviled ham; then roll jelly roll style, beginning on the long side of the oblong. Wrap in waxed paper, and chill in the refrigerator. While dough is chilling, preheat oven to 400 degrees. Prepare a baking pan with spray-oil. When dough is completely chilled, cut in 1/2-inch slices, and place rolls on the pan. Bake in the preheated oven for 20 to 30 minutes until the rolls become a light golden; do not brown. Serve hot or room temperature. Makes 18.

May also be served as an appetizer.

Jalapeno Corn Bread

This recipe is somewhat lighter than other recipes for the same type dish.

1-1/4 cups plain corn meal
1/2 cup plain flour
1 tablespoon granulated sugar
1 tablespoon baking powder
1/2 teaspoon salt
3 egg whites, beaten
1 whole egg, beaten

1 cup skim milk
8 oz. cream style corn
4 oz. grated light Jarlsberg cheese or sharp Cheddar cheese
1 (4-oz.) can chopped green chilies, with juice
1/4 cup chopped onions
1/2 to 1 small fresh jalapeno pepper, minced, or 4 pickled jalapeno slices, minced
3/4 cup canola oil

Preheat oven to 450 degrees. Prepare a 9- x 13-inch baking pan with spray-oil. In a small bowl, mix corn meal, flour, sugar, baking powder, and salt. In a large bowl, beat the remaining ingredients; then add the corn meal mixture to the milk mixture until just barely moistened. Place the baking pan in the preheated oven for a couple of minutes to get hot; then pour in the corn bread batter. Bake in the preheated oven for 30 minutes or until done. Serve hot, cut in squares.

Sweet Potato Biscuits

2 scant cups sweet potatoes, cooked and whipped (do not use canned) 2-1/2 cups self-rising flour 1 cup granulated sugar	Pinch of salt 1/4 teaspoon baking soda 1/2 cup vegetable shortening 1/4 cup milk

Bake the sweet potatoes in the oven or microwave until very soft. Peel and whip the sweet potatoes; set aside. In a large bowl, mix the flour, sugar, salt, and soda together; then blend in the shortening until very well mixed. Stir in the whipped sweet potatoes; then slowly add milk to form a ball. Preheat oven to 400 degrees. The biscuits can be spoon-dropped or kneaded lightly on a floured board to cut out. If cutting out, roll 1/2-inch thick with a floured rolling pin. Cut with a small biscuit cutter, and place on a spray-oil prepared baking pan. Bake in the preheated oven for 12 to 15 minutes.

This biscuit mixture can be made and refrigerated for several days. When ready to bake, follow baking instructions above.

Light Corn Bread With Whole Wheat

This recipe is a low-cholesterol, low-fat recipe for corn bread. 1 cup whole wheat flour 1 cup self-rising corn meal 4 teaspoons baking powder	1 tablespoon granulated sugar 1 cup skim milk 2 egg whites, beaten 2 tablespoons canola oil 1/4 teaspoon salt

Preheat oven to 425 degrees. In a large bowl, mix whole wheat flour, corn meal, baking powder, and sugar. Add milk, egg whites, oil, and salt; mix to blend. Prepare an 8- x 8-inch pan with spray-oil; then pour in the batter. Bake in the preheated oven for 20 minutes or until done. Cut into squares, and serve hot.

Sweet Breads

Strawberry Pecan Bread

Makes 2 loaves and can be served with or without frosting.	4 eggs
	1 cup vegetable oil
	1/2 cup sour cream
3 cups plain flour	1 teaspoon lemon juice
2 cups granulated sugar	2 cups frozen strawberries,
1 teaspoon salt	thawed and drained
1 teaspoon baking soda	1-1/4 cups pecans, chopped

Frosting:	
	1/4 cup frozen strawberries,
8 oz. cream cheese, softened	thawed and drained

Preheat oven to 350 degrees. Measure flour and sift; then re-measure flour by spooning lightly into cup. Re-sift flour with the dry ingredients; set aside. In an electric mixer, beat the eggs very well; then beat in the oil, sour cream, and lemon juice. Add the flour mixture, a small amount at a time; then continue to beat for an additional 2 minutes. Add strawberries and pecans until just blended. Prepare 2 loaf pans by spraying with Baker's Joy; then pour the batter evenly divided in the 2 pans. Bake in the preheated oven for 50 to 60 minutes or until done. Allow to cool 10 minutes before turning out on wire racks to cool completely.

Frosting: In an electric mixer, whip the cream cheese with the strawberries until light and fluffy. Spread loaf tops when cooled.

Apple pecan muffins

2 cups plain flour
1/2 cup light brown sugar, packed
2 teaspoons baking powder
1 teaspoon baking soda
1/2 teaspoon salt
1 cup buttermilk
1/4 cup vegetable oil

1 large egg
2 to 4 Granny Smith apples,
   peeled, cored, and shredded
   (2 cups)
1/2 cup pecans, chopped
1 tablespoon granulated sugar
1/2 teaspoon cinnamon

Preheat oven to 400 degrees. Prepare 12 full-size muffin cups with spray-oil. Using a large bowl, sift together the flour, brown sugar, baking powder, soda, and salt. In a small bowl using a fork, beat buttermilk, oil, and egg until well blended. Stir the liquid mixture in the flour mixture until flour mixture is moistened only; batter will be lumpy. Fold in apples and pecans. In a cup, mix granulated sugar and cinnamon. Spoon batter in muffin cups; then sprinkle with cinnamon sugar mixture. Bake muffins in the preheated oven for 25 minutes or until they test done. Immediately remove from pan to a wire rack. Serve warm or cool. Makes 12.

Old Fashioned Gingerbread

3/4 cup vegetable shortening	1 cup buttermilk
1 cup granulated sugar	3-1/2 cups plain flour
2 eggs	4 teaspoons ground ginger
1 cup molasses	1 teaspoon salt
2 teaspoons baking soda	

Scrumptious Sauce:	1/2 cup reserved gingerbread batter from recipe above
Optional, but with the name of the sauce, and the story below, could you possibly resist?	2 cups hot water
	1/2 cup granulated sugar
	2 tablespoons butter

Preheat oven to 350 degrees. In an electric mixer, cream the shortening, while slowly adding the sugar, until light and fluffy. In a separate bowl, beat the eggs by hand; then beat in the molasses. In a cup, dissolve the soda in the buttermilk, and blend. Sift together the flour, ginger, and salt. Alternate, adding all three mixtures to the shortening mixture; beat an additional 2 minutes. If using the sauce recipe below, reserve 1/2 cup of the batter to be used in the sauce. Prepare a 9- x 13-inch baking pan with spray-oil. Pour batter in pan, and bake in the preheated oven for 30 minutes or until done. Serve plain or with the sauce.

Sauce: In a heavy saucepan, stir the hot water in the batter until blended. Add sugar and butter; cook slowly, stirring constantly, until the sauce is as thick as desired. Serve sauce warm over warm gingerbread.

Both of the above recipes are Ellis family treasures. The gingerbread came from Gladys Ellis, a favorite aunt. The sauce was developed by Grandmother Ellis, Ellen Hagood Ellis, to use less sugar. In earlier days when sugar was hard to get, Grandmother Ellis made this sauce for different cakes, instead of making icing. Try it; it's a prize winner!

Raspberry Pecan Sweet Bread

Makes 2 loaves.

3 cups plain flour
1 teaspoon baking soda
1 teaspoon salt
2 cups granulated sugar

3 eggs
1-1/4 cups vegetable oil
20 oz. frozen raspberries, thawed
1-1/4 cups pecans, chopped

Preheat oven to 350 degrees. Measure flour, and sift; then re-measure flour by spooning lightly into cup. Re-sift flour with soda, salt, and sugar. In an electric mixer, beat the eggs; then beat in the oil. Slowly add the flour mixture to blend. Fold the raspberries and pecans in by hand. Prepare 2 loaf pans with Baker's Joy spray-oil; then pour the batter evenly in the pans. Bake in the preheated oven for 1 hour and 15 minutes or until done. Allow to cool 20 minutes before turning out of pans.

A grand combination of flavors, both sweet and tart.

Sweet Orange Rolls

2 cups plain flour	1 teaspoon grated orange rind
2 tablespoons granulated sugar	1/3 cup milk
2 teaspoons baking powder	1/3 cup orange juice
1/2 teaspoon salt	12 small cubes sugar
4 tablespoons vegetable 　　shortening	Additional 1/4 cup orange juice

Preheat oven to 375 degrees. Measure flour, and sift; then re-measure flour by spooning lightly into cup. Then re-sift flour with sugar, baking powder, and salt. In a bowl, cut the shortening and orange rind into the flour mixture with a fork or a pastry cutter until very well mixed. Gradually add the milk and the 1/3 cup orange juice until a soft dough is formed. Roll out dough on a lightly floured board to 3/4-inch thickness. Prepare a cookie sheet with spray-oil, and place biscuit rounds on the pan. Dip the sugar cubes, one at a time, in the 1/4 cup orange juice. Place 1 sugar cube on each biscuit. Bake in the preheated oven for about 15 minutes. Makes 12.

Nutty Apple Bread

2 cups plain flour	2/3 cup granulated sugar
1 teaspoon baking powder	2 eggs
1/2 teaspoon baking soda	1-1/2 cups peeled, cored,
1/2 teaspoon salt	shredded Granny Smith
1 teaspoon ground nutmeg	apples
1/2 cup margarine, softened	1 cup pecans, chopped

Preheat the oven to 350 degrees. Measure flour, and sift; then re-measure flour by spooning lightly into cup. Re-sift flour with baking powder, baking soda, salt, and nutmeg; set aside. In an electric mixer, cream the margarine and sugar until light; add eggs, 1 at a time. Beat until mixture is light and fluffy. Slowly beat in the flour mixture, and beat for an additional 2 minutes. By hand, stir in the apples and pecans until blended. Prepare a loaf pan with spray-oil. Pour batter in loaf pan, and bake in the preheated oven for 50 to 60 minutes or until done. Allow to cool for 20 minutes; then turn out of pan on a cooling rack. Cool completely before slicing.

The candy caper

*E*arly in the 1950's Priester's Pecan Company purchased an existing small handmade candy company in Montgomery, Alabama. Since it proved inconvenient to run businesses in two cities, the candy-making business was moved to Fort Deposit, to be part of the pecan mail-order business.

*T*wo of the candy makers were hired to move to Fort Deposit to teach the pecan company employees the "candy-making ropes." These two must have decided that they would not be staying with the pecan company unless they made themselves indispensable. They proceeded to scramble the ingredients and instructions for making all of the candy recipes. And batch after batch had to be thrown away. The former candy company owner was called and tried to unscramble the recipes to no avail.

*T*he sugar saboteurs were packed off and were fortunately replaced by a loyal employee, Jewel "Cookie" Cook. She tested and re-tested candy recipes in that first tiny kitchen, containing a stove, one large copper kettle, and a small marble table. "I prayed and cried many a night, and the good Lord directed me," she said.

*J*ewel was as proud of the company's products as L. C. and Hence, the owners. She could not have given more to the success of Priester's had it been her own company. Such loyalty bears remembering.

Cakes

Toasted Butter Pecan Cake

1-1/3 cups pecans, chopped	2 cups granulated sugar
1 cup plus 2 tablespoons butter, divided	4 eggs
3 cups plain flour	1 cup buttermilk
2 teaspoons baking powder	1 teaspoon vanilla
1/2 teaspoon salt	Suggested frosting: Caramel or Dark, Dark Chocolate Glaze

In a 350 degree oven, toast the pecans in 2 tablespoons of the butter for 20 to 25 minutes. Watch carefully and stir often; ovens vary, and pecans can overcook quickly! Keep oven preheated. Measure flour, and sift; then re-measure flour by spooning lightly into cup. Re-sift flour with baking powder and salt; set aside. In an electric mixer, cream the remaining 1 cup butter and sugar until light. Add eggs one at a time, and beat well after each egg. Add flour mixture a small amount at a time, alternating with the buttermilk and vanilla. Beat batter an additional 2 minutes. By hand, stir in the toasted pecans. Prepare 3 cake layer pans by spraying with Baker's Joy. Pour the batter, divided evenly, in the three pans. Bake in the preheated oven for 25 to 30 minutes. Allow cakes to cool in pans for 15 minutes before turning out of pans. Cool cakes completely before frosting.

This is a fabulous tasting cake that is excellent even without a frosting.

May's Caramel Icing

Use a candy thermometer. Assemble and measure all ingredients, and have all utensils handy before beginning recipe. Even place ice cubes in a large metal container before beginning recipe.

2-1/2 cups granulated sugar, divided	1 teaspoon vanilla
1/2 cup margarine, melted	Ice cubes
3/4 cup milk	1 cup pecans, chopped (to be
1 egg, well beaten	added after icing is spread on cake)

In a heavy, large saucepan, mix 2 cups of the sugar with the melted margarine. Beat in the milk and egg. Begin heating the mixture over medium heat; then place the remaining 1/2 cup sugar in an iron skillet. Begin heating and stirring the sugar in the skillet, while also stirring the milk mixture. Allow the sugar to completely melt and turn a light golden color. Immediately remove skillet from the heat. At this point, the milk mixture should be hot, but not boiling. Beat the melted sugar in the milk mixture; and cook with a candy thermometer in the icing to a temperature of 238 degrees. Immediately remove saucepan from heat, and allow to cool for a few seconds while beating in the vanilla. Place saucepan in the ice-filled container in sink, and beat the icing to a consistency just short of being too hard to pour. If icing should become too stiff add a few drops of cold milk to thin the icing. Pour icing on cake or cakes; then sprinkle with the pecans. Ices 1 large cake or 3 layer cakes.

May Green Ellis, one of the Priester's Pecan Company owners, makes this fantastic "real" caramel icing - - a much sought-after delicacy. I had always heard this was a difficult recipe to make, but had received many requests for it. Since I had never made it myself, I prevailed upon May to be kind enough to step me through the successful making of her Caramel Icing. Now you too, can "wow 'em all!"

Tropical Snowstorm Cake by Karen

Filling Step 1:	1/2 cup granulated sugar
2 cups water	1/4 cup grated orange rind

Filling Step 2:	2 tablespoons butter
1 cup granulated sugar	2 tablespoons lemon juice
1/4 cup cornstarch	2 tablespoons reserved orange
1/4 teaspoon salt	rind from Step #1
1 cup orange juice	

Cakes:	2 cups granulated sugar
	3 egg yolks
2 cups plain flour	3/4 cup milk
2 teaspoons baking powder	2 egg whites, room temperature
1/4 teaspoon salt	2 tablespoons reserved orange
3/4 cup butter, softened	rind from Step #1

Topping:	2 teaspoons Myers Dark Rum
	(optional)
1/2 pint whipping cream	10 oz. or more frozen grated
1/3 cup granulated sugar	coconut, thawed

Filling Step #1: In a small saucepan, combine the water and sugar; bring to a boil. Add the orange rind; then gently boil for 3 minutes. Pour the mixture in a fine strainer, or through cheese cloth to capture the cooked orange rind. Discard the liquid. Set aside the cooked rind to divide between the filling and cake batter.

Filling Step #2: In a medium saucepan, combine the sugar, cornstarch, and salt. Gradually stir in the orange juice, and bring to a boil. Lower heat to medium, and stir until thickened. Remove from heat; and stir in the butter, lemon juice, and 2 tablespoons of the reserved orange rind. Allow filling to completely cool. (Continued on next page)

Tropical Snowstorm Coconut Cake by Karen
(Continued)

Cakes: Preheat oven to 350 degrees. Prepare two 9-inch round cake pans with spray-oil; then line with waxed paper. Measure flour, and sift; then re-measure flour by spooning lightly in cup. Re-sift flour with baking powder and salt; set aside. In an electric mixer, cream the butter with the sugar until light. Add egg yolks, one at a time, beating after each addition. Gradually beat in the flour mixture, alternating with the milk. Beat an additional 2 minutes. In a separate small bowl, beat the egg whites until stiff peaks form. Fold beaten egg whites with the remaining reserved orange rind into the batter. Pour batter in the cake pans; then trim the excess waxed paper from the pans. Bake in the preheated oven for 25 to 30 minutes. Allow cakes to cool for 10 minutes; then remove cakes to cool completely on a wire rack. Peel waxed paper from the cakes. When cakes are completely cooled, slice each cake in half horizontally.

Topping: In a small chilled bowl, whip the cold whipping cream to form soft peaks. Gradually beat in the sugar; then beat in the rum. The coconut is used in the next step.

Cake assembly: Spread the filling between each 1/2 layer of cake and stack. Spread the top layer and sides with the whipped cream topping; then sprinkle the thawed coconut on the top and sides. Refrigerate cake for several hours before cutting. Keep cake refrigerated. Cake may be frozen.

Karen Newton with the able assistance of Lonnie Carden, our hiking and paddling cohorts, have made this luscious cake for our Christmas night dinners for several years. Our whole family thinks it's "The Best." It is a special occasion cake. Time consuming to make, yet you'll find your time most appreciated. Karen's friend Leila gave her the recipe several years ago, and now we can all enjoy it.

Genia's Coconut Whipped Cream Cake

1 (18.5-oz.) box white cake mix	14 to 16 oz. frozen coconut,
12 oz. sour cream	thawed and divided
2 cups granulated sugar,	2 pints whipping cream
plus extra	

Make cakes as directed on the package for layer cakes. Cool cakes completely; then slice horizontally. In large bowl, mix the sour cream, sugar, and 10 oz. of the coconut for the cake filling. Reserve 1/2 cup of the filling; set aside. Spoon filling in a thick layer between each 1/2 layer, allowing it to run down the side. Using a chilled bowl and beaters for an electric mixer, whip the cream until stiff; then sweeten with extra sugar to taste. By hand, mix in the reserved 1/2 cup filling; then ice the entire cake. Sprinkle the remaining coconut over the entire cake. Refrigerate to chill before cutting. Keep refrigerated.

Unbelievably good. If there's any left after the first cutting, refrigerate. Joe Westbrook has been known to virtually wipe-out a large portion of the cake single-handedly, and I won't even mention the damage I can do!

Chocolate Decadence Frosting

1/2 cup butter or margarine,	1/8 teaspoon salt
softened	4 tablespoons hot, strong coffee
1 lb. powdered sugar, sifted	1 cup pecans, chopped
5 tablespoons cocoa	

In an electric mixer, cream the butter or margarine, powdered sugar, cocoa, and salt. Add just enough hot coffee to make the frosting a spreading consistency. By hand, stir in the pecans.

Almand's Favorite Italian Cream Cake

Cake:
2 cups plain flour
5 large eggs, separated and room
   temperature
2 cups granulated sugar, divided
1 cup margarine, softened

1/2 teaspoon salt
1 teaspoon baking soda
1 cup buttermilk
1 cup pecans, chopped
4 oz. frozen or fresh grated
   coconut, thawed

Frosting:
1/2 cup margarine, softened
8 oz. cream cheese, softened
1 to 1-1/4 lbs. powdered sugar,
   sifted

1/2 cup pecans, chopped
Additional pecan halves to
   decorate

Cake: Preheat oven to 325 degrees. Prepare three cake layer pans with Baker's Joy. Measure flour, and sift; then re-measure flour by spooning lightly into cup. Re-sift flour; set aside. In an electric mixer, beat the egg whites until they form soft peaks; then slowly add 1/2 cup of the sugar. Set aside. In another electric mixer bowl, cream margarine, remaining sugar, and salt. Add egg yolks, one at a time, until well blended. In a cup, stir the soda in the buttermilk. Alternate, adding buttermilk mixture to the batter with the flour; scrape bowl sides until well blended. Fold egg whites into batter with a large spoon until lightly mixed; do not beat. By hand, gently stir in the pecans and coconut until barely mixed. Pour the batter evenly in the pans. Bake in the preheated oven for 30 to 40 minutes or until cakes test done. Allow cakes to cool for 25 minutes; then turn out of pans. Cool completely before frosting.

Frosting: In an electric mixer, cream margarine and cream cheese. Add powdered sugar until a good spreading consistency is achieved. By hand, stir in the pecans. Frost layers and sides; then decorate with pecan halves.

The first time I made this cake for my family, my son Almand announced that he would have to very carefully reconsider his annual birthday cake request. Many years later, it's still #1 for him.

Melissa's Mandarin Orange Cake

1 (18.25-oz.) package orange or pineapple flavor cake mix 1/2 cup vegetable oil	4 eggs 1 (11-oz.) can mandarin oranges with juice

Frosting:

1 (15-1/4-oz.) can crushed pineapple 1 (16-oz.) carton whipped topping 1 (3.4-oz.) box vanilla instant pudding mix	1 cup pecans, chopped Pecans halves to decorate (optional) Extra mandarin orange slices to decorate (optional)

Cake: Do not follow cake package instructions, except for preheating oven temperature. In an electric mixer, beat the cake mix, oil, eggs, and undrained mandarin oranges for 4 minutes. Prepare 3 layer cake pans with Baker's Joy. Pour the batter evenly in the 3 pans, and bake in the preheated oven for the time listed on the cake package directions. Allow cakes to cool 15 minutes before turning out of pans; then cool cakes completely. While cakes are cooling, drain the pineapple for the frosting using a colander. *Frosting:* In a large bowl, mix all frosting ingredients with the drained pineapple. Refrigerate the frosting until cakes are cooled. Frost tops of cakes, and stack the layers; then frost the entire cake. Decorate the entire cake with pecans halves, and extra mandarin orange slices, if desired. Refrigerate the cake for several hours before cutting. Keep cake refrigerated.

This fruit flavored cake serves a small army, and that seems to be needed for all of the men in Melissa's life. Melissa Casey and Thomas Ellis, owners of Priester's Pecan Company, have three very active, growing young men, hungry for one of Mama's homemade cakes. Then again, Thomas can hold his own with the guys when it comes to sweets!

Priester's Whipped Cream and Pecan Cake

6 eggs, separated and room temperature	1 teaspoon vanilla
1-1/2 cups granulated sugar, divided	3 cups Priester's pecan meal, divided
2-1/2 tablespoons plain flour (yes, tablespoons!)	1 pint whipping cream
	Extra powdered sugar for cream
1 teaspoon baking powder	Sweet wine to flavor cream
1/2 teaspoon salt	(optional)

Preheat oven to 350 degree. In an electric mixer, beat the egg whites until very stiff; then add 1/4 cup of the sugar. In a separate electric mixer bowl, beat the egg yolks with the remaining sugar for 5 minutes on medium speed. Sift the flour, baking powder, and salt; add to the egg yolks. Beat in the vanilla; then slowly add 2-1/2 cups of the pecan meal until well blended. By hand, gently fold in the stiffly beaten egg whites until all ingredients are barely mixed. Prepare two 9-inch cake layer pans with Baker's Joy. Pour the batter evenly in the 2 pans, and bake in the preheated oven for 20 to 25 minutes or until cakes test done. Allow cakes to cool for 15 minutes; then turn out of pans on wire racks to cool completely. When cakes are thoroughly cooled, whip the cream in an electric mixer until stiff; then flavor with sugar and a small amount of sweet wine to taste. Spread the sweetened whipped cream on the tops of both cake layers, and stack. Sprinkle the top layer with the remaining pecan meal. Refrigerate cake.

This is truly "old world" decadence made easy with an electric mixer. Can you only imagine whipping the eggs and cream with a fork? Thank you Mr. Edison!

Winnie's Kahlua Cake

There are two choices. The Kahlua Cake; or a lightened and shortened version. Both are terrific.

Cake:

1 (18.5-oz.) box chocolate cake mix	1/2 cup water
	1/2 cup vegetable oil
1 (3-oz.) package instant chocolate pudding mix	1/2 cup Kahlua
	4 eggs

Frosting:

	1-1/2 lbs. powdered sugar, sifted
3/4 cup margarine (1-1/2 sticks), softened to room temperature	2 to 4 tablespoons Kahlua
	6 to 8 tablespoons milk
6 tablespoons cocoa	1 cup pecans, chopped

Cake: Preheat oven to 325 degrees. In an electric mixer, beat all of the above cake ingredients, ignoring the ingredients called for on the cake package. Prepare 3 round layer pans with Baker's Joy. Divide the batter evenly among the pans, and bake in the preheated oven for 25 to 30 minutes or until cakes test done. Allow cakes to cool for 15 minutes before turning out of pans. Cool completely before frosting.

Frosting: In an electric mixer, cream the margarine, cocoa, and powdered sugar; then gradually add the Kahlua. Beat to mix; then add just enough of the milk to make the frosting a good spreading consistency. Frost each layer top, and sprinkle with pecans. Stack the 3 layers to make the cake; then frost the cake sides without pecans.

Winnie's Skinny Kahlua Cake

Cake:	
1 box Betty Crocker Sweet Rewards Reduced Fat Chocolate Cake Mix	1/4 cup Kahlua

Frosting:	6 tablespoons cocoa
	1-1/2 lbs. powdered sugar, sifted
3/4 cup light margarine (1-1/2 sticks), softened to room temperature	2 to 4 tablespoons Kahlua
	6 to 8 tablespoons skim milk
	1 cup pecans, chopped (optional)

Cake: Preheat oven to 325 degrees. Prepare the cake according to the cake directions; then beat in the Kahlua. Prepare 3 round layer pans with Baker's Joy. Divide the batter evenly among the pans, and bake in the preheated oven for 25 minutes or until cakes test done. Allow cakes to cool for 15 minutes before turning out of pans. Cool completely before frosting.

Frosting: In an electric mixer, cream the margarine, cocoa, and powdered sugar; then gradually add the Kahlua. Beat to mix; then add just enough of the skim milk to make the frosting a good spreading consistency. Frost each layer top, and sprinkle with pecans, if desired. Stack the 3 layers to make the cake; then frost the cake sides without pecans.

*Winnie Long and her daughter, Ginny Hudson, make this coffee-lovers dream cake. Ginny and her husband, John, have fed many a great meal to their friend and my son, Almand. Thus saving him from the **DREADED** "Mystery Meat" and "Fish Portions" served in the cafeteria, when he was a student at Auburn University. Doctor and Mrs. Long have entertained both of our sons at their lake home on Lake Hartwell in South Carolina. Both of the guys came home talking about the Kahlua Cake.*

Genia & Mandy's Favorite Grecian Orange Cake

Cake:	
1 (18.5-oz.) box yellow cake mix	4 eggs
1 (3.5-oz.) package instant lemon pudding mix	3/4 cup water
	3/4 cup vegetable oil

Glaze:	1/2 cup plus 2 tablespoons frozen orange juice concentrate
2 cups powdered sugar, sifted	2 tablespoons margarine, melted

Cake: Do not use cake box instructions. Preheat oven to 325 degrees. In an electric mixer, mix all cake ingredients on low speed for 1 minute; then mix for 2 minutes on medium speed. Scrape sides constantly during the mixing process. Prepare a Bundt or tube pan with Baker's Joy. Pour the cake batter in the pan, and bake in the preheated oven for 45 minutes or until cake tests done.

Glaze: In a medium saucepan, mix all glaze ingredients; then stir, and cook over low heat until completely dissolved, about 3 minutes. Set glaze aside until cake is baked. When cake has finished cooking, remove from oven. Leaving the cake in the pan, carefully pierce the cake, almost to the bottom, with an ice pick or bamboo skewer. Pour the hot glaze over the hot cake; then allow the cake to completely cool, while still in the pan. When cake is cold, turn out of pan onto a plate; then immediately invert cake onto a cake platter, in order to have the glaze side up.

This cake was made by the grandmother of my daughter's close friend and college roommate, Mandy Pope Smith. A care package with Grecian Orange Cake had to be carefully guarded in a dorm full of hungry girls. The algebra's forgotten, but they still remember the Grecian Orange Cake.

Nancy's "Regular" Sour Cream Pound Cake

3 cups plain flour
1/2 teaspoon salt
1/4 teaspoon baking soda
3 cups granulated sugar
8 oz. butter, softened (no
   substitutes)

6 eggs, room temperature
1 cup sour cream
2 teaspoons almond or lemon
   extract
1 teaspoon vanilla extract

Preheat oven to 325 degrees. Measure flour, and sift; then re-measure flour by spooning lightly into cup. Re-sift flour with salt and soda; then sift a third time. Sift the sugar 3 times. In an electric mixer, cream butter and sugar until very light. Add eggs, one at a time, mixing between each addition. Alternate adding the flour mixture with the sour cream, beginning and ending with the flour. Add both extracts, and mix. Prepare a Bundt or tube pan with Baker's Joy; then pour in the batter. Bake in the preheated oven for 1 hour and 10 minutes or until cake tests done. Cool 40 minutes before turning out of pan.

This recipe comes with a precious story. Nancy and A. B. Carlan's little two-year old granddaughter, Hannah Carlan, was visiting their home. She went into Nancy's kitchen and asked for a piece of cake. Nancy asked which kind of cake, since she had several cakes already baked. Little Miss Hannah stood there and thought and thought; then with a big smile she announced "Regular." It seems that around the Carlan household the Sour Cream Pound Cake is considered the "Regular Cake."

"War Eagle"
Pound Cake by Cis

3 cups plain flour	1 (8-oz.) package cream cheese,
Pinch of salt	softened
3 cups granulated sugar	6 eggs
1-1/2 cups (3 sticks) butter,	1 tablespoon vanilla
softened	(yes, tablespoon!)

Cake begins in a COLD oven.   Measure flour, and sift; then re-measure flour by spooning lightly into cup. Re-sift flour with salt; set aside. Sift the sugar 3 times; then cream the sugar with the butter and cream cheese in an electric mixer until very light. Add eggs, one at a time, beating after each addition. Gradually beat in the flour mixture and the vanilla. Beat an additional 2 minutes. Prepare a full-size Bundt or tube pan with Baker's Joy. Pour the batter in the pan, and place in a cold oven, yelling "War Eagle" loudly when you close the door. Turn oven to 300 degrees, and bake for 2 hours or until cake tests done. Allow cake to cool for 45 minutes before turning out of pan.

I can only assume that this very cake can be made successfully by shouting other epithets, such as "Roll Tide," "Go Gators," "Vols," "Noles," "Dawgs," "Navy," "Army," "Nittany Lions," "Aggies." I know, I know--I haven't mentioned YOUR team yet!   Please forgive; space doesn't permit.

Orange Pecan Date Cake

2 cups plain flour	1 teaspoon baking soda
1/2 cup butter, softened	2/3 cup buttermilk
1 cup granulated sugar	1 cup pecans, chopped
2 eggs	1/2 cup chopped dates

Glaze:	
Juice of 2 large fresh oranges or 3 tablespoons prepared orange juice	1/2 cup granulated sugar Grated rind of 1 orange (optional)

Preheat oven to 350 degrees. Measure flour and sift; then re-measure flour by spooning lightly into cup. Re-sift flour and set aside. In an electric mixer, cream butter and sugar until light; then add eggs, one at a time. Continue to beat until light and fluffy. Stir the soda in the buttermilk until blended; then add the buttermilk mixture to the batter. Gradually add the flour to the batter, and mix an additional 2 minutes. By hand, stir in the pecans and dates until blended. Prepare a Bundt or tube pan with Baker's Joy. Pour in the batter, and bake in the preheated oven for about 30 minutes or until cake tests done. While cake is baking, prepare the glaze by mixing all ingredients in a small saucepan. Heat and stir until the sugar is dissolved; set aside. When cake is done, remove from oven, and loosen the edges while cake is hot and still in the pan. Pour cake glaze over the hot cake in the pan, and return to the oven for 3 minutes. Remove cake from oven, and allow to cool in the pan for 20 minutes before turning out of pan.

An heirloom recipe handed down through the Ellis family for many years. It is most unusual and delicious.

Too Good Chocolaty Cupcakes

4 squares unsweetened chocolate	1 cup plain flour
1 cup butter or margarine	4 eggs, beaten
1/4 teaspoon butter flavoring	1 teaspoon vanilla
1-1/2 cups pecans, chopped	1/8 teaspoon salt
1-3/4 cups granulated sugar	

Preheat oven to 325 degrees. In a small heavy saucepan, melt the chocolate and the butter. Add butter flavoring and the pecans; stir to coat. Remove saucepan from the heat. In a large bowl, combine the sugar, flour, eggs, vanilla, and salt until just barely mixed; do not beat. Gently stir the chocolate mixture in the sugar mixture without beating. Place foil-lined baking cups in 18 muffin tin cups, and evenly divide the batter in the cups. Bake in the preheated oven for 30 to 40 minutes or until cupcakes test done.

Pineapple Pecan Bars

2 cups plain flour	1/2 teaspoon salt
2 cups brown sugar, packed	1 egg
1/2 cup margarine, softened	3/4 cup sour cream
1 cup pecans, chopped	1 teaspoon vanilla
1/2 teaspoon ground cinnamon	8 oz. crushed pineapple, drained
1 teaspoon baking soda	

Preheat oven to 350 degrees. In an electric mixer, beat together the flour, brown sugar, and margarine until crumbly. By hand, stir in the pecans. Prepare a 9- x 13-inch baking pan with Baker's Joy. Remove 2 cups of the crumbly mixture, and press in the bottom of the pan. To the remaining crumbly mixture in the bowl, add the cinnamon, baking soda, and salt. Beat in the egg, sour cream, and vanilla until well blended. Stir in the drained pineapple; then spread the pineapple mixture over the crumbly mixture. Bake in the preheated oven for 30 to 35 minutes until bars pull away from the sides. Allow to cool slightly before cutting into bars.

Salley ♥'s Chocolate Pound Cake

3 cups plain flour	1 cup vegetable shortening
1/2 teaspoon baking soda	4 eggs
1 teaspoon salt	2 teaspoons vanilla
1 (4-oz.) bar Baker's German	2 teaspoons butter flavoring
Sweet Chocolate	1 cup buttermilk
2 cups granulated sugar	

Preheat oven to 300 degrees. Measure flour and sift; then re-measure flour by spooning lightly into cup. Re-sift flour with the soda and salt; set aside. In a double boiler, partially melt the chocolate bar over boiling water; then remove from heat, and stir rapidly until completely melted. Allow chocolate to cool. In an electric mixer, cream the sugar and shortening until light. Add eggs, one at a time, and beat until light and fluffy. Beat in the vanilla, butter flavoring, and buttermilk until blended. Slowly beat in the flour mixture; then beat for an additional 2 minutes. Stir in the melted chocolate until well blended. Prepare a Bundt or tube pan with Baker's Joy. Pour the batter in the pan, and bake in the preheated oven for 1 and 1/2 hours or until cake tests done. Immediately remove cake from pan, and place the cake under a tight-fitting cover until the cake is thoroughly cooled. Frost cake with Dark, Dark Chocolate Glaze (see recipe below.)

Dark, Dark Chocolate Glaze

10 oz. semi-sweet chocolate chips	1/2 pint whipping cream

In the top of a double boiler over boiling water, combine the chocolate chips and the whipping cream. Allow chips to melt, while stirring the cream, until mixture is completely blended. Remove top portion of the double boiler, and allow the glaze to cool for 15 minutes.

This is a glaze that flows freely over cake layers. It is dark, semi-sweet, and decadent. Sorry, I'm beginning to sound like Emily writing Wuthering Heights! Nevertheless it has a cliff-hanging flavor! This has gotta be the easiest thing to make to be so good.

Alabama Lane Cake

Make at least one day in advance. Raisins must be soaked 1 hour in advance.

Cake:
3-1/4 cups plain flour
2 teaspoons baking powder
1/2 teaspoon salt
1 cup butter or margarine,
    softened

2 cups granulated sugar
1 cup milk
1 teaspoon vanilla
8 egg whites

Filling:

1 cup golden raisins
1 cup bourbon
8 egg yolks
1 cup granulated sugar

1/2 cup butter or margarine,
    very soft
1 teaspoon vanilla
1 cup pecans, chopped
1 cup frozen grated coconut,
    thawed (optional)

Seven Minute Frosting:

2 egg whites
1-1/2 cups granulated sugar
1/4 cup plus 1 tablespoon water
1-1/2 teaspoons white corn syrup
1/4 teaspoon cream of tartar

1 teaspoon vanilla
Additional ingredients may be
    used and added at the same
    time as the vanilla, such as:
    chopped pecans, dried fruit
    tidbits, thawed frozen grated
    coconut, food color tint, etc.

Cake: Preheat oven to 375 degrees.   Measure flour and sift; then re-measure flour by spooning lightly into cup. Re-sift flour with baking powder and salt; set aside. In an electric mixer, cream butter and sugar until light. Alternate adding the milk, vanilla, and flour mixture, beginning and ending with the flour. In a separate bowl, beat the room temperature egg whites until very stiff. Gently fold the egg whites in the cake batter until just barely blended. Using 3 cake layer pans, prepare pans with Baker's Joy. Pour the batter evenly divided in the 3 pans; bake in the preheated oven for 25 to 30 minutes or until cakes test done. After baking, allow cakes to cool 20 minutes before turning out of pans; cool cakes completely before frosting.   (Continued on next page)

Alabama Lane Cake
(continued)

Filling: After soaking the raisins in the bourbon for 1 hour, begin the filling. In an electric mixer, beat the egg yolks until a light lemon color. Slowly add the sugar and the soft butter until well blended. In a double boiler over boiling water, cook the filling until thick, stirring constantly. Add the raisins with the bourbon, vanilla, and pecans. Stir to mix; then immediately remove the top of the double boiler to allow filling to begin to cool. Cool completely before spreading between cake layers. If using the coconut, it will be used later in the cake assemble step.

Frosting: Be very careful while making this frosting since it requires using a mixer over boiling hot water. Place the double boiler top over boiling water in the base pot. Beat all of the frosting ingredients, except vanilla and any additions with a rotary or electric beater for seven minutes or until frosting stands in peaks. Remove from boiling water; add vanilla, and continue beating until frosting is a good spreading consistency. Add any additional ingredients selected at this time.

Cake Assembly: After cake layers are cool, spread the cooled filling evenly between 2 of the layers; then sprinkle each layer with the coconut, if desired. Place the remaining layer on top, and frost the entire cake. Refrigerate cake overnight before cutting; keep cake refrigerated.

This is an old Southern tradition-style cake, especially used for holidays. The cake will be almost too "bourbony" just after making. It needs to be refrigerated overnight for the flavors to spread throughout the cake layers. Then you will definitely not find it too "bourbony" to eat! Although you may need a designated driver after a couple of slices!

Fresh From the Tree Pear Cake

2-1/2 cups plain flour	3 eggs
1 teaspoon baking soda	1 cup vegetable oil
1 teaspoon salt	1 teaspoon vanilla
2 teaspoons baking powder	3 cups peeled, finely diced,
2 teaspoons ground cinnamon	fresh pears
2 cups granulated sugar	1 cup pecans, chopped

Preheat oven to 350 degrees. Measure flour and sift; then re-measure flour by spooning lightly into cup. Re-sift flour with baking soda, salt, baking powder, and cinnamon. In an electric mixer, beat the sugar with the eggs; then slowly add the oil, and beat 1 minute. Gradually add the flour mixture to the egg mixture until well blended. Beat in the vanilla, and continue to beat on medium speed for 2 minutes. By hand, fold in the pears and pecans. Prepare a 9- x -13-inch baking pan with Baker's Joy. Pour batter in the pan, and bake in the preheated oven for 45 to 50 minutes or until cake tests done. Cool cake for 10 minutes; then turn out on a wire rack to cool completely. This allows the cake bottom to air properly. Cut in squares to serve.

When your lawn is being "bombed" by all the pears on your very prolific pear tree, this is the perfect, delicious solution to your "problem."

Susan's 49'ers

2 cups Bisquick biscuit mix	2 cups pecans, chopped
1 lb. light brown sugar, packed	Powdered sugar for dusting
4 eggs, well beaten	

Preheat oven to 325 degrees. In a large bowl, combine all ingredients, except powdered sugar, until very well blended. Prepare a 9- x 13-inch baking pan with Baker's Joy. Pour batter in pan, and bake in preheated oven for 25 to 30 minutes. After removing from oven, dust with powdered sugar, and allow to cool completely before cutting in squares.

Peaches & Cream Cake

Chop peaches before measuring.

1 (18.5-oz.) package Duncan Hines Butter Recipe Golden Cake Mix	1/2 cup water
	1 pint whipping cream
	3 tablespoons sifted powdered sugar
1-1/2 cups granulated sugar	1 cup sour cream, divided
4 tablespoons cornstarch	Fresh or frozen peach slices for decoration
4 cups chopped peaches, fresh or frozen	

Prepare cake according to package directions, using 2 cake layer pans. Allow cakes to cool in pan for 20 minutes. Turn cakes out of pans, and allow to cool completely. When layers are cold, split each layer in half horizontally. The layers may be trimmed of the dome-tops to make layers level for stacking. In a medium saucepan, combine the sugar and cornstarch; then add the peaches and water. Cook over medium heat, stirring constantly, until the mixture is smooth and very thick. Allow the peach mixture to cool completely. In an electric mixer, whip the cream to stiff peaks, and add the powdered sugar to taste. Place a split cake layer on a cake plate; then spoon 1/3 of the peach filling over the layer, and spread over the tops only. Spread 1/3 cup sour cream over the peach filling; repeat layers, ending with a cake layer. Frost the final cake layer with the sweetened whipped cream, and decorate the top with the peach slices.

Diane's Fantastic Fresh Apple Squares

2-1/2 cups plain flour	2 eggs
2 teaspoons baking powder	1 teaspoon vanilla
1 teaspoon salt	1 cup pecans, chopped
1 teaspoon baking soda	3 cups peeled, shredded Granny
1-1/2 cups vegetable oil	Smith apples
2 cups granulated sugar	

Preheat oven to 350 degrees. Measure flour and sift; then re-measure flour by spooning lightly into cup. Re-sift flour with the baking powder, salt, and soda; set aside. In an electric mixer, combine the oil and sugar; then add the eggs, one a time, beating after each addition. Beat in the vanilla; then slowly add the flour mixture, and beat for an additional 2 minutes. By hand, fold in the pecans and apples until mixed. Prepare a 9- x 13-inch baking dish with spray-oil; then pour in the batter. Bake in the preheated oven for 55 minutes or until cake tests done. After cake has cooled, cut in squares.

One of my very favorite apple cakes. I like the Granny Smith apple taste, both sweet and tart.

Cream Cheese Pecan Frosting

8 oz. cream cheese, softened	1 lb. powdered sugar, sifted
1/2 cup margarine	1 cup pecans, chopped

In an electric mixer, cream all ingredients except pecans until smooth. Add pecans by hand, and stir to mix. Frosts 3 layer cakes or 1 large Bundt or tube cake.

chocolate
Raisin Squares

2 cups plain flour
2 cups granulated sugar
1/4 teaspoon salt
1/2 teaspoon cinnamon
1/2 cup margarine, softened
1/2 cup vegetable shortening
2 (1-oz.) squares unsweetened
  chocolate

1/2 cup water
1/2 cup raisins, chopped
1 cup buttermilk
1 teaspoon baking soda
2 large eggs

Frosting:

1/2 lb. powdered sugar, sifted
Pinch of salt
1/4 cup margarine, softened

3 tablespoons milk
1 (1-oz.) square unsweetened
  chocolate
3/4 cup pecans, chopped

Preheat oven to 375 degrees.   Measure flour and sift; then re-measure flour by spooning lightly into cup. Re-sift flour with sugar, salt, and cinnamon in an electric mixer bowl. In a saucepan, add margarine, shortening, chocolate, water, and raisins; bring to a boil. Immediately pour boiling mixture over the flour mixture; then beat on medium speed until well blended. In a cup, combine buttermilk and soda; then add to the batter. Beat in eggs, one at a time. Prepare a 9- x 13-inch baking pan with Baker's Joy, and bake in the preheated oven for 30 minutes. Frost while still in the pan and hot.

Frosting: Sift together the powdered sugar and salt. In a saucepan, bring to a boil the margarine, milk, and chocolate. Remove from heat, and vigorously beat in the sugar mixture until smooth. Add pecans, and pour over the hot cake; spread evenly. Cut in squares to serve. Makes 20 to 24 squares.

Cookies

Russian Cream Cookies favored by Marsha, Bill, Anna, & Reynolds Cook

1 tablespoon hot water	2 eggs
1 teaspoon baking soda	1 teaspoon vanilla
1 cup margarine, softened	4 cups plain flour
1-1/2 cups light brown sugar, packed	1 cup raisins
	1 cup pecans, chopped

Preheat oven to 325 degrees. In a small bowl, stir the hot water in the soda; and set aside. In an electric mixer, cream margarine and sugar until light. Add eggs, and continue to cream until light and fluffy. Add the soda mixture and the vanilla until well blended. Add the flour, a small amount at a time, until completely mixed. By hand, stir in the raisins and pecans. Prepare cookie sheets with spray-oil. Drop batter by spoonfuls to 50 cent size. Bake in the preheated oven for 12 to 15 minutes.

An often-used cookie recipe of Marsha Ellis Cook and her mother May Green Ellis, owners of Priester's Pecan Company. The recipe has been made and handed down through at least 3 appreciative generations.

Aunt Kathleen's Famous Family Favorite Cookies

3 egg whites, room temperature	3 tablespoons plain flour
1-1/2 cups light brown sugar, lump free	3 cups pecan halves

Preheat oven to 225 degrees. In an electric mixer, beat the egg whites until very stiff and dry. Gradually beat in the brown sugar. Sift flour; then re-measure, and add flour to the egg white mixture. By hand, stir in the pecan halves until coated. Prepare a cookie sheet with spray-oil, and drop cookies by teaspoonfuls far enough apart to prevent touching. Bake in the preheated oven for about 25 minutes or until cookies are lightly browned, slide on the pan, and do not make a finger impression when touched.

Kathleen Ellis Ryals, sister of Mr. Hence, the co-founder of Priester's Pecan Company, has made these very light, crunchy cookies for gifts for all of the Ellis and Ryals children for 3 generations. They have become a much-sought-after family tradition. Miss Kathleen moved into "The Big House," on the cover of this cookbook, as a very young child.

Miss Kathleen's son, Dr. Jarvis Ryals of Pueblo, Colorado, has recently given a donation for the Frank and Kathleen Ellis Ryals School of Public Health Building at the University of Alabama in Birmingham. His generosity honors his parents and promotes the health of all. Such philanthropy deserves our recognition and thanks.

Cowboy Cookies
Devoured by Tyler, Stinson, and Taber Ellis

2 cups plain flour	2 eggs
1 teaspoon baking powder	1 teaspoon vanilla
1/8 teaspoon salt	1-1/2 cups granola cereal
1/2 teaspoon baking soda	1-1/2 cups cornflakes
1 cup margarine	1 cup uncooked quick oats
1 cup light brown sugar, packed	1 cup flaked, canned coconut
1 cup white granulated sugar	1 cup pecans, chopped

Preheat oven to 325 degrees. In a large bowl, sift the flour, baking powder, salt, and baking soda. In an electric mixer, cream the margarine and both sugars. Add eggs, one at a time, and the vanilla. Gradually beat in the flour mixture until well blended. By hand, stir in both of the cereals, oats, coconut, and pecans. Prepare cookie sheets with spray-oil. Drop cookies by spoonfuls to 50 cent size. Bake in the preheated oven for 10 to 12 minutes. Makes about 90 to 100 cookies.

Leonard's Pecan Wafers

1 lb. pecans	2 egg whites, room temperature
1 cup unsalted butter, softened	1/4 cup plain flour
1 cup granulated sugar	1/4 teaspoon salt

Preheat oven to 350 degrees. Spread the pecans in a large, ungreased baking pan in a single layer. Watching carefully, toast pecans until lightly browned; allow to cool completely. After pecans are cool, place in a food processor with a steel blade; turn on and off several times to lightly mince the pecans. Do not make or use pecan meal; it is too fine. In an electric mixer, cream the butter until light; then add sugar, a little at a time, until light and fluffy. Add egg whites, one at a time; then beat until mixture is smooth. In another bowl, blend the ground pecans, flour, and salt. By hand, gently fold the pecan mixture in the batter until barely blended. Prepare several cookie sheets with spray-oil; then drop mixture by teaspoonfuls at least 2-inches apart on the cookie sheets. If cookies are too close together, they will spread into one big cookie! Bake in the preheated oven about 10 minutes or until wafers are golden brown. After baking, immediately remove the cookies to cool on racks. Makes 60.

German Nut Cookies by Sara

1 egg	1 teaspoon vanilla
1 cup margarine, melted	2 cups plain flour
1 cup granulated sugar	1 cup pecans, chopped

Preheat oven to 250 degrees. Separate the egg, and allow to come to room temperature. In an electric mixer, beat the margarine, sugar, vanilla, egg yolk, and flour. Spread very thin on an ungreased cookie sheet. In another electric mixer bowl, beat the room temperature egg white very stiff and dry. Spread the stiff egg white over the cookie mixture (will be very thin,) and sprinkle with the pecans. Bake in the preheated oven for 1 and 1/2 hours or until golden brown. Cut cookies in squares immediately.

Scottish Millionaire Shortbread

Shortbread:	
1/4 cup caster sugar (see instructions below to caster)	5 oz. plain flour (1/2 cup plus 1 tablespoon)
1/2 cup margarine	

Topping:	
1/2 cup margarine	1 (14-oz.) can sweetened condensed milk
1 teaspoon light corn syrup	1 (8-oz.) bar milk chocolate
1/4 cup caster sugar	Chopped pecans (optional)

Shortbread: Caster the sugar for both the shortbread and the topping at the same time. Using a food processor with the steel blade or a blender, place granulated sugar in the container. Blend the sugar until it is finer than granulated, but not as fine as powdered sugar; then measure the castered sugar. Preheat the oven to 350 degrees. In a food processor or an electric mixer, cream the margarine, 1/4 cup caster sugar, and flour into a dough. Press the dough in a thin layer in the bottom of a 9- x 13-inch ungreased baking pan. Bake in the preheated oven for about 12 minutes until golden brown. Allow to cool completely before topping.

Topping: In a medium saucepan, melt the margarine; then add the syrup, 1/4 cup caster sugar, and condensed milk. Heat and stir to boiling; then allow to boil for another 4 to 5 minutes, stirring constantly. Pour the hot mixture over the cooled shortbread, and set aside to cool. When the topping is completely cool, melt the chocolate in a double boiler over boiling water. Drizzle or spread the melted chocolate over the topping, and sprinkle with pecans, if desired. Refrigerate to allow chocolate to set before cutting in squares. Keep refrigerated.

carmelitas

Cookies:	1/4 teaspoon salt
	3/4 cup light brown sugar
1-1/2 cups plain flour	1-3/4 cups quick oats
1/2 teaspoon baking soda	3/4 cup margarine, melted

Topping:	1 (6-oz.) package milk or semi-sweet chocolate chips
1 (10-oz.) package caramel candies, unwrapped	1 cup pecans, chopped
	Reserved oat mixture from cookie dough above
1/4 cup water	

Cookies: Preheat oven to 350 degrees. In a large bowl, mix the flour, baking soda, and salt. Stir in the brown sugar, and mash to remove all sugar lumps; then mix in the oats. Stir in the melted margarine until well blended. Measure 1-1/3 cups of the oat mixture, and reserve for the topping. Prepare a 9- x 13-inch baking dish with spray-oil. Press the non-reserved oat mixture in the bottom of the baking pan. Bake in the preheated oven for 10 minutes. Allow to cool completely.

Topping: In a medium saucepan, melt the unwrapped caramels with the water, and stir to mix. Sprinkle the chocolate chips and pecans over the top of the cooled pan of cookies. Drizzle the hot caramel mixture over the chocolate chips and pecans, leaving a 1/4-inch edge with no caramel. Top with the reserved oat mixture. Bake in the preheated oven for 15 to 18 minutes or until golden brown.

This recipe was given to me with highest praise from Jo, Joy, and Kimberly Mikell. It was served to them on a skiing vacation in Canada. I can now understand why they raved so much over the Carmelitas, but I can't understand why they didn't take me on their ski trip! Actually we WERE invited; but alas, the writing of this cookbook took precedence over a ski trip. Oh, the woes of a working woman!

Victorian Lemon Wafers

1/2 cup butter or margarine, softened	1 cup plus 2 tablespoons plain flour
3/4 cup granulated sugar	1-1/2 teaspoons lemon extract
2 eggs	Small pecan halves

Preheat oven to 350 degrees. In an electric mixer, cream butter; then gradually add sugar, beating until light. Add eggs, one at a time; then beat in flour and lemon extract. Prepare several cookie sheets with spray-oil. The wafers spread while baking and will flow together for one huge cookie if not properly spaced! Drop batter in very small amounts by level teaspoonfuls on baking sheets, at least 2-inches apart. Place pecans in center of wafers. Bake in preheated oven for 6 to 8 minutes or until cookie edges are browned. Immediately remove hot baked wafers to a wire rack to cool; do not stack. As soon as wafers are completely cooled and crisp, place in tightly sealed containers; wafers become soggy very quickly in humid conditions. Makes about 5 dozen.

Pecan Tassies

Crust:	1/2 cup margarine, softened
3 oz. cream cheese, softened	1-1/2 cups sifted self-rising flour

Filling:	1 teaspoon vanilla
1 egg	Pinch of salt
1 cup light brown sugar, packed	1 cup pecans, chopped & divided

Preheat oven to 350 degrees. In an electric mixer, beat cream cheese and margarine; then mix in flour until well blended. Refrigerate for 1 hour. Prepare mini-muffin tins with spray-oil. After dough has chilled, form dough into 24 small balls, and press the dough balls against the bottom and sides of mini-muffin tin cups. In a bowl, beat the egg, brown sugar, vanilla, and salt until well blended; then stir in 2/3 cup of the pecans. Spoon filling into dough-lined cups; then top with remaining pecans. Bake in the preheated oven for 15 minutes or until firm. Remove from muffin tins immediately, and allow to cool. Makes 24.

Smoky Mountain cookies by Sherie

2-1/2 cups quick oats	1 cup butter or margarine
2 cups plain flour	1 cup light brown sugar, packed
1 teaspoon baking powder	1 cup granulated sugar
1 teaspoon baking soda	2 eggs
1/2 teaspoon salt	1 teaspoon vanilla
4 oz. Hershey's chocolate bars, refrigerated	1 (12-oz.) package chocolate chips
	1/2 cup pecans, chopped

Preheat oven to 350 degrees. Measure the oats, and place in a small bowl. Using a food processor with a steel blade or a blender, pulverize small amounts of the oats until all oats are powdered. In a large bowl, sift the flour, baking powder, baking soda, and salt. Stir in the powdered oats until well blended. Coarsely grate the cold Hershey's chocolate bars; then place in a cool area. In an electric mixer, cream the butter and both sugars. Add eggs, one at a time, beating between each addition; then beat in the vanilla. Slowly beat in the flour/oat mixture until blended. By hand, stir in the chocolate chips, grated chocolate bars, and pecans; mix well. Prepare a 9- x 13-inch baking dish with spray-oil. Roll the cookies into golf ball-size rolls. Place cookies on baking pan at least 2-inches apart, to give spreading room. Bake in the preheated oven for about 12 to 14 minutes. Immediately remove cookies from baking pan to a wire rack to cool. Cookies should cool separately, not stacked. Makes 50 cookies.

These beyond-wonderful cookies will give you the energy to hike up and down the gorgeous, high Smoky Mountains, savoring them to the fullest. From the trillium and spring beauties wild flower carpets in spring; to mountain laurel, flame azaleas, and rhododendron in early summer; on to breath-taking arrays of autumn leaf colors; and then into delicate russet colors exposed on snowy winter days. It's hard to tell which I love the most, the mountains or the cookies!

Swedish Heirloom Cookies

1/2 cup margarine, softened	1 teaspoon vanilla
1/4 cup granulated sugar	1 cup ground pecans or meal
1 cup self-rising flour	3/4 cup powdered sugar

Preheat oven to 300 degrees. In an electric mixer, cream margarine and granulated sugar until light. Gradually add all remaining ingredients except powdered sugar. Roll balls the size of a quarter; then flatten with palm of hand to 50-cent size. Place on ungreased cookie sheet, and bake in preheated oven for 20 to 25 minutes. Remove from oven, and allow to cool for 5 minutes. Place powdered sugar in a clean plastic bag; then drop several slightly cooled cookies in bag, and shake to coat cookies with powdered sugar. Makes 24 cookies.

Karen's Southern Creams

Cookies:	3 eggs, well beaten
5 cups plain flour	1 teaspoon vanilla
1 teaspoon salt	1 cup sour cream
3 teaspoons baking powder	1-1/2 cups pecans, chopped
1/2 teaspoon baking soda	*Topping:*
1 cup margarine	3 tablespoons granulated sugar
2 cups granulated sugar	1 teaspoon cinnamon

Preheat oven to 350 degrees. Measure flour, and sift with salt, baking powder, and baking soda. In an electric mixer, cream margarine and sugar. Beat in eggs, vanilla, and sour cream. Gradually beat in flour mixture until well blended. By hand, stir in pecans. Prepare cookie sheets with spray-oil, and drop by spoonfuls to 50-cent size. In a small bowl, mix topping ingredients. Grease bottom of a small, thick glass. Dip bottom of glass in topping mixture; then very carefully press cookies flat with glass. Bake in the preheated oven for 12 to 15 minutes. Makes 6 to 7 dozen cookies.

Karen Rennekamp is a native of Nebraska but a Southerner by choice! She's an outstanding hostess; you'll enjoy these cookies.

Santa's Whiskers

Make several hours or overnight before baking time.

1 cup margarine
1 cup granulated sugar
2 tablespoons milk
1 teaspoon vanilla or rum extract

2-1/2 cups plain flour
3/4 cup (combined) red and
   green candied cherries
1/2 cup pecans, finely chopped
3/4 cup flaked, canned coconut

Preheat oven to 375 degrees. In an electric mixer, cream the margarine and sugar. Gradually beat in the milk, vanilla or rum extract, and flour. By hand, stir in the cherries and pecans until well mixed. On waxed paper, form the mixture in two rolls about 2-inches in diameter and 8-inches long. Sprinkle the coconut along the outside of the rolls, and gently pat to affix the coconut, but not "bury" it. Place the rolls in a flat, covered container, and refrigerate for several hours or overnight. Cut the cold cookie rolls with a warm-blade knife or electric knife in 1/4-inch slices. Bake on an ungreased cookie sheet in the preheated oven for about 12 minutes or until edges are golden. Makes 50 to 60.

Rugalach

An easy version of the recipe for an ancient Jewish pastry cookie.

1/2 cup dark raisins	1 teaspoon ground cinnamon
2 oz. pecan, walnut, or almond meats	1 folded commercial refrigerator pie crust
1 tablespoon granulated sugar	Powdered sugar to sprinkle

Place an oven rack in center of the oven. Preheat oven to 425 degrees. In a food processor or blender, combine raisins, nuts, sugar, and cinnamon. Blend, using the on-off switch, to finely chop, but not pulverize, mixture. Unfold pie crust on a lightly floured board. With a rolling pin, roll pastry thinner; retaining the round shape. Cut crust in 16 equal wedges. Divide raisin mixture evenly over each wedge. Roll each wedge, beginning with wide edge toward the point. Prepare a baking pan with spray-oil. Place pastries with the point side down, and gently form into a crescent. Bake in preheated oven for 8 to 10 minutes or until golden. Remove pastries to a wire rack to cool; then lightly sprinkle tops with powdered sugar.

Mocha Munchies

No cooking involved for this recipe.	1 lb. powdered sugar, sifted
1 large, commercial angel food cake	3 tablespoons prepared strong coffee
3/4 cup margarine (1-1/2 sticks)	2 tablespoons brandy or rum (optional)
2 teaspoons instant coffee	2 cups finely chopped pecans (more if needed)
Few drops water	

Cut entire angel food cake in 1-inch cubes. In a medium saucepan, melt margarine. Dissolve instant coffee in a few drops of water, and add to margarine. Stir in powdered sugar, prepared coffee, and brandy; mix well. Place pecans in a clean plastic bag. Using a long-handled, 2-prong kitchen fork, skewer each cube; then gently dip in coffee icing. Drop iced cubes of cake in the bag with pecans, and shake to coat cubes. Refrigerate munchies until serving time. Keep refrigerated.

chocolate cherry peek cookies

1-1/2 cups plain flour	1 egg
1/2 cup cocoa	1 teaspoon vanilla
1/4 teaspoon salt	1 (10-oz.) jar maraschino
1/4 teaspoon baking powder	cherries, with juice
1/4 teaspoon baking soda	6 oz. semi-sweet chocolate chips
1/2 cup margarine, softened	1/2 cup sweetened condensed
1 cup granulated sugar	milk

Preheat oven to 350 degrees. In a medium bowl, mix the flour, cocoa, salt, baking powder, and baking soda. In an electric mixer, cream the margarine and sugar. Beat in the egg and vanilla until light and fluffy. Gradually beat in the flour mixture until well blended. Form dough in 1-inch balls, and place on an ungreased cookie sheet. Press thumb in the top of each cookie to make an indentation for the cherry. Drain the cherry juice in a bowl, and reserve liquid; remove cherry stems. Place a whole or a half cherry on each cookie. In a small saucepan, heat the chocolate chips and condensed milk over low heat until chocolate is melted. Stir in 2 teaspoons of the reserved cherry juice. Spoon 1 teaspoonful of frosting around the edge of each cherry, leaving a small area of red cherry peeking out in the center of each cookie. Bake the cookies in the preheated oven for about 10 minutes. Makes 40 cookies.

Linda Sparks, my sister by marriage, makes these luscious and decadent cookies. I must thank my brother for having the good sense to marry such a sweet, charming, and pretty lady.

Pies

Priester's Perfect Pecan Pie

3 eggs	1/4 teaspoon salt
1/2 cup granulated sugar	1 teaspoon vanilla
1/2 cup light brown sugar, packed	1-1/3 cups pecans, chopped or
1/2 cup light corn syrup	halves
1/4 cup margarine or butter,	1 folded commercial refrigerator
melted	pie crust, unbaked
1 teaspoon white vinegar	

Preheat oven and a baking pan to 350 degrees. In a large bowl, lightly beat the eggs; then beat in both sugars, corn syrup, melted margarine, vinegar, salt, and vanilla until well blended. Pour the pecans in the unbaked pie crust; then pour the egg mixture over the pecans. Bake on the preheated baking pan in the preheated oven for 35 to 40 minutes. Filling should be slightly firm and the top browned.

Joe's Blackberry Cobbler

3/4 cup granulated sugar
4 tablespoons cornstarch
1/8 teaspoon salt
2 (16-oz.) cans blackberries in
   heavy syrup, undrained

1 tablespoon margarine
2 folded commercial refrigerated
   pie crusts, unbaked

Preheat oven and a baking sheet to 375 degrees. In a saucepan, combine the sugar, cornstarch, and salt; mix well with a fork. Gradually stir in the juice from both cans of the undrained blackberries until mixture is smooth. Cook and stir over medium heat until mixture is thick and clearer in color. Add margarine, and stir until blended; then add blackberries. Unfold and fit 1 pie crust in a deep-dish pie plate. Pour pie filling in the unbaked crust. Unfold the remaining unbaked pie crust; flatten and roll with a rolling pin until crust is thinner. Cut the thinner pastry in long strips, and lattice the top of the pie with the strips. Bake on the preheated baking sheet in the preheated oven for 40 minutes.

Now this is really scary. My husband, Joe, actually came up with this recipe! He loves blackberry cobbler. Since fresh blackberries are only available once a year, he decided to experiment with canned blackberries. It is a fantastic recipe, which I can highly recommend. Sometimes his kitchen creations are nuclear meltdowns. His line of expertise usually runs to the more exotic technical pursuits such as flying an airplane at over 500 miles an hour, designing and building a photography darkroom, or fabricating a piece of equipment from scratch. Usually, cooking minute rice is a hardship, not to mention finding the mayonnaise in the refrigerator.

Scotty's Lemon Pie

Pie requires 2 to 24 hours standing time.	2 cups granulated sugar
	2 folded commercial refrigerator pie crusts, unbaked
2 large fresh lemons, washed	4 eggs, well beaten

Slice the whole lemons tissue-paper thin. Remove seeds from slices, and discard both end pieces. Place slices in a small to medium glass mixing bowl, and add sugar. Stir to mix lemon slices and sugar. Cover bowl, and allow to stand, unrefrigerated, for 2 hours (may stand as long as 24 hours, if refrigerated.) Preheat oven and a baking sheet to 450 degrees. After standing time, line a 9-inch pie dish with 1 of the pie crusts. In a large bowl, vigorously beat the eggs until well beaten; then beat in the sugared lemon slices until very well mixed. Pour mixture in pie crust; then arrange lemon slices evenly over the bottom. Place the second pie crust on top; press the two pie crust edges together, and flute. Cut 10 small slits in top of crust in an attractive design to allow steam to escape. Bake on the preheated baking pan in the preheated 450 degree oven for 15 minutes; then reduce heat to 375 degrees, and bake an additional 20 minutes.

My sister, Scotty Sparks, is a very special person. She is a day student at the Louise Maytag Smith Center for adult special education. She loves the Center and all of her instructors. Scotty has the wisdom of Einstein, yet the charming, loving innocence of the young. She also has the memory of an elephant, so don't even try to let a birthday slip by unnoticed. She always remembers!

chocolate Earthquake pie

Makes two pies.

1 cup margarine
1 cup semi-sweet chocolate chips
4 eggs
2 cups granulated sugar
Pinch of salt

1-1/4 cups pecans, chopped
1 cup frozen grated coconut,
    thawed
2 folded commercial refrigerator
pie crusts, unbaked

Preheat oven and a baking sheet large enough to hold 2 pies to 350 degrees. In the top of a double boiler over boiling water, melt the margarine and chocolate chips; set aside. In a bowl, beat the eggs very well; add sugar, salt, pecans, and coconut until well mixed. Stir in the chocolate mixture. Pour evenly in the pie crusts, and bake on the preheated baking sheet for 40 to 45 minutes or until set. Makes 2 pies.

When this pie bakes, the top crust cracks like the earth during a Richter scale 7.5 earthquake! Tastewise, it is definitely a shaker and a mover! It is one of my all-time-favorite pies. Of course, all you have the say to me is "chocolate," and I'll like it!

old-fashioned cheese cake
by Katrina

Crust:

8 oz. graham cracker crumbs or
 1-1/2 individual packages
 graham crackers crushed

2 tablespoons granulated sugar
4 tablespoons butter or
 margarine, melted

Filling:

3 (8 oz.) packages cream cheese,
 softened
1-1/2 cups granulated sugar
16-oz. sour cream

1 (14-oz.) can sweetened
 condensed milk
2 tablespoons lemon juice
2 teaspoons vanilla
8 eggs

Crust: Preheat oven to 325 degrees. Crush graham crackers, and add sugar. Using a 10-or 14-inch springform pan, mix the sweetened graham crackers with the melted butter. Press down, and form a graham cracker crust on the bottom of the pan, and partially up the sides of the pan.

Filling: In an electric mixer, beat the cream cheese, sugar, sour cream, milk, lemon juice, and vanilla. Beat in the eggs, one at a time, until the mixture is thoroughly blended and smooth. Pour filling in the crust. Bake in the preheated oven for 1 hour and 10 minutes. After this baking time, turn off the oven. Keep door to the oven shut for an additional 1 hour. Remove cheesecake from oven after the additional 1 hour, and allow to cool to room temperature; then refrigerate.

This cheesecake also freezes very well.

Lord Oxford of Lazy Acres
Triple Decker Cherry Pie

Makes 2 pies. One for the dog, and one for you (read below!) Prepare at least 4 hours before serving time.

Crust:	
	1/2 cup margarine, melted
1-1/2 cups plain flour, sifted	1/3 cup pecans, finely chopped

First Deck:	Third Deck:
11 oz. cream cheese, softened	2 (1 lb.-5-oz.) cans cherry pie
1 cup powdered sugar, sifted	filling
2 tablespoons milk	1 pint whipping cream, well
Second Deck:	chilled
1 cup pecans, coarsely chopped	2 tablespoons granulated sugar

Crust: Preheat oven to 375 degrees. In an electric mixer, combine all 3 ingredients to form a dough. Prepare 2 pie plates by spraying with spray-oil; then press dough evenly to form crust on bottoms and 1/2 way up sides. Bake in the preheated oven for 20 minutes; allow to cool for 1 hour.

First Deck: In an electric mixer, cream the 3 ingredients until blended. Spread 1/2 of mixture on each cooled pie crust.

Second Deck: Sprinkle the pecans on both pies.

Third Deck: Spread 1 can of cherry pie filling on each pie. In an electric mixer, whip cream, and add sugar. Spoon whipped cream over both pies. Refrigerate for at least 4 hours before serving; keep refrigerated. Serves 16.

Well, it was a lovely sunny afternoon, and my new daughter and son, Melody and Jay, were helping me test this recipe for this cookbook. They were invited to a friend's home for dinner that night, so I gave them one of the pies to take as the dessert. Melody placed the pie in their automobile back seat and returned to our house for another item. In a split-second, our large black labrador, Lord Oxford of Lazy Acres, retrieved the pie from the back seat of the car and devoured it in one big gulp! He didn't even drop a cherry on the car seats. When Melody returned a few seconds later, Oxford was smiling and licking his cherry-red chops.

Lola's Chocolate Pecan Angel Pie

Make the pie early on a sunny day. The pie does not make properly when there is too much moisture in the air.

Shell:	1 teaspoon vanilla
	1/4 teaspoon salt
2 egg whites, room temperature	2/3 cup granulated sugar
1/8 teaspoon cream of tartar	1/2 cup pecans, chopped

Filling:	1/4 cup water
	1/2 pint whipping cream
1 (6-oz.) package semi-sweet	3 tablespoons granulated sugar
chocolate chips	1/2 teaspoon vanilla

Shell: Preheat oven to 275 degrees. In an electric mixer, beat the room-temperature egg whites until peaks begin to form. Beat in the cream of tartar, vanilla, and salt. Gradually add sugar, and continue beating until very stiff peaks form. By hand, fold in the pecans. Prepare a 9-inch pie dish with spray-oil. Spoon the egg mixture in the dish to cover the bottom, and as much of the sides as possible. Do not cover rim itself. Bake in the preheated oven for 1 and 1/2 to 2 hours or until light golden brown and crisp. Allow shell to cool completely.

Filling: In a double boiler over boiling water, melt the chocolate chips and water. Do not stir until chocolate pieces are completely melted; then stir until smooth. Remove mixture from heat, and allow to cool. In an electric mixer, beat the cream until stiff; then add sugar and vanilla. By hand, fold in the melted chocolate. Spoon the chocolate mixture in the cooled shell, and refrigerate for 4 hours or overnight.

Fresh Strawberry Pie by Von

1 folded commercial refrigerator pie crust (9-inch)
2 pints fresh strawberries
3/4 cup granulated sugar
2 tablespoons cornstarch

4 tablespoons strawberry Jello powder
1 cup water
Whipped topping

Bake the pie crust according to package directions, and allow to cool completely. Remove hulls, wash, and drain the strawberries; then slice into a small bowl. In a medium saucepan, mix the sugar, cornstarch, Jello powder, and water. Heat to boiling, and cook until the liquid becomes clear. Place sliced strawberries evenly in the cooled pie crust, and pour the hot sauce over the strawberries. Refrigerate for several hours until well chilled, or overnight. When ready to serve, cut pie in wedges. Top each pie slice with a dollop of whipped topping. Serves 6 to 8.

Strawberry lovers don't pass this up. It's so very easy, eye-appealing, and scrumptious! Von Jones is a home economics teacher, and a lovely lady who knows her profession!

Chocolate Rum Frozen Pie

Make one day in advance.

1/2 gallon vanilla ice cream
1/4 cup chocolate syrup plus extra

1-1/2 oz. rum
1 cup toasted pecans, chopped
2 chocolate cookie pie crusts
12 pecan halves

Soften ice cream enough to stir in the chocolate syrup; then stir in rum and pecans. Pour in the cookie crusts, and freeze. After pies are frozen, decorate the tops with pecan halves, and drizzle more of the chocolate syrup in swirls around the pecans. Cover with the plastic pie lids from the cookie crusts, and freeze overnight. Makes 2 pies.

I'm almost reluctant to tell how quickly this dessert can be made!

John K's favorite
Lemon pecan chess pie

2 cups granulated sugar
1 tablespoon plain flour
1 tablespoon self-rising corn meal
4 eggs, lightly beaten
1/4 cup milk
2 to 4 tablespoons grated
   lemon rind

1/4 cup lemon juice
1/2 cup chopped pecans, divided
1 commercial folded refrigerator
   pie crust, unbaked

Preheat oven to 350 degrees. Combine sugar, flour, and corn meal in a large bowl. Toss lightly with a fork. Add eggs, milk, lemon rind, lemon juice, and 1/4 cup of the chopped pecans. Beat with an electric mixer until smooth and thoroughly blended. Pour in unbaked pie crust; sprinkle remaining 1/4 cup pecans over top. Bake in preheated oven for 35 to 40 minutes or until top is golden brown.

Carolyn's
Cream Cherry Cheese Pie

Makes 2 pies with no baking.
1/3 cup granulated sugar
12 oz. cream cheese
8 oz. sour cream
8 oz. whipped topping

1 teaspoon vanilla
2 graham cracker crumb pie
   crusts
2 (1 lb.-5-oz.) cans cherry pie
   filling

In an electric mixer, beat the sugar and cream cheese; then add the sour cream, whipped topping, and vanilla. Beat until smooth. Spread 1/2 of the cream cheese mixture in one pie shell; then repeat with the other pie shell. Top with one can of the cherry filling per pie. Spread evenly over the pie tops. Refrigerate until completely chilled before cutting. Serves 14 to 16.

Peanut Butter Pie by Amy

1 cup powdered sugar	2 cups milk
1/2 cup creamy peanut butter	3 eggs, separated and room
1 baked pie shell, cooled	temperature
1/4 cup cornstarch	2 tablespoons margarine
2/3 cup granulated sugar	1/4 teaspoon vanilla
1/4 teaspoon salt	

Preheat oven to 325 degrees. In a food processor or blender, combine the powdered sugar and peanut butter. Blend until the consistency of coarse corn meal. Spread 1/2 of the peanut butter mixture in the cooled, baked pie shell. In a medium saucepan, combine cornstarch, sugar, and salt; mix to blend. In another saucepan, heat the milk until hot but not boiling. Gradually stir the hot milk into the sugar mixture until the mixture is smooth. Cook over low heat, stirring constantly, until thickened. Beat egg yolks in a small bowl; then SLOWLY add a SMALL amount of hot mixture into the egg yolks to bring yolks to cooking temperature. Add egg yolk mixture to sugar mixture slowly, and cook, stirring for 2 minutes. Remove from heat, and stir in margarine and vanilla. Allow to cool slightly; then spoon the filling mixture over the first layer. Sprinkle 1/2 only of the remaining peanut butter mixture over the filling, reserving the remaining 1/2 as a topping. In an electric mixer, beat the egg whites until very stiff. Spread egg white mixture over the top, and sprinkle with the remaining peanut butter mixture. Bake in the preheated oven for 20 minutes or until firmly set and lightly browned. Allow to cool before serving.

Thomas Ellis, one of the owners of Priester's Pecan Company, highly recommends this pie. He and his wife, Melissa, asked their friend Amy Killingsworth to share her recipe with all of us. Amy, you've really pulled off quite a coup; getting a "pecan man" to request a peanut recipe!

Ina Rosser's Sweet Potato Pie

2 cups cooked, mashed sweet
  potatoes
1 cup granulated sugar
1 tablespoon plain flour
1/4 cup margarine, melted
1/3 cup milk

2 eggs, lightly beaten
1-1/2 teaspoons real vanilla
  extract
1/2 teaspoon lemon extract
1 folded commercial refrigerated
  pie crust, unbaked

Preheat oven and baking pan to 400 degrees. In a large mixing bowl, combine all ingredients, except the pie crust. Mix until well blended. Pour the sweet potato mixture in the pie crust; then place the pie on the preheated baking pan in the preheated oven. Bake for 10 minutes; then reduce the heat to 350 degrees. Bake until pie crust is lightly browned and filling is set.

Sweet potato pie is an old, traditional Southern pie. Somehow my family never got the message; although they are all dyed-in-the-wool Southerners. Guess that train passed them by! This recipe was given to me by Sherie Rosser Wilson, a friend. It was her grandmother Ina Rosser's recipe and was baked for all of their family gatherings for as long as Sherie can remember. Miss Ina lived 81 wonderful years, so the recipe is quite old.

Dorothy's Praline Cheesecake

Crust:	
1-1/4 cups graham cracker crumbs	1/4 cup pecans, chopped and toasted
1/4 cup granulated sugar	1/4 cup margarine, melted

Filling:	2 tablespoons plain flour
3 (8-oz.) packages cream cheese	1-1/2 teaspoons vanilla
1 cup brown sugar, packed	3 eggs
1 (5-1/3-oz.) can evaporated milk	1 cup pecan halves, toasted

Sauce:	
1 cup dark corn syrup	2 tablespoons brown sugar
1/4 cup cornstarch	1 teaspoon vanilla

Crust: Preheat oven to 350 degrees. In a small bowl, combine graham cracker crumbs, sugar, and pecans. Stir in melted margarine to make a crumb mixture. Using a 10-inch springform pan, press crumb mixture to form a crust on bottom, and 1-1/2-inches up sides of pan. Bake in preheated oven for 10 minutes. Allow crust to completely cool.

Filling: In an electric mixer, beat cream cheese, brown sugar, evaporated milk, flour, and vanilla. Beat in eggs, one at a time, until just blended. Pour in cooled crust, and bake in preheated oven for 50 to 55 minutes or until set. Cool in pan for 30 minutes; then loosen sides, and remove rim from pan. Allow to cool completely. Arrange pecan halves on top of cooled cake.

Sauce: Prior to serving, make sauce in a small saucepan. Combine corn syrup, cornstarch, and brown sugar. Over medium heat, cook and stir until thickened and bubbly. Remove from heat; then stir in vanilla. Allow to cool slightly; then spoon a portion of warm sauce over top of cheesecake. Pour extra sauce in a pitcher to serve on the side. Makes 12 to 16 servings.

The instructions say that this will make 12 to 16 servings, but Dorothy Harris Kuerner, or "Teedy," my sister by marriage, declares that it only serves one, when you are having a "bad hair day." Sounds like a good excuse to me, and to Julie, Jessica, Jill, and Dan Kuerner. Thanks, Teedy, for the extraordinary taste treat.

Sugar & Spice

Cupid's Heart Apple Tart

1 sheet of a (17-1/4-oz.) package frozen puff pastry dough	1/4 cup granulated sugar
1 egg, well beaten	1 tablespoon water
3 Granny Smith apples	1 thin slice of lemon
	1 pint fresh strawberries, sliced

Preheat oven to 400 degrees. Place unfolded and thawed pastry sheet on a lightly floured board. With a rolling pin, roll the pastry to a slightly larger size. Cut one 6-inch heart out of puff pastry. Cut 1/2-inch wide strips of pastry from remaining dough. Brush edges of heart with beaten egg. Twist pastry strips, and line the edges of the heart with the strips. Use all pastry to make the lip deep. Join all edges of strips with egg as necessary. Bake in the preheated oven according to package directions. When heart is golden and fully baked, remove from oven, and press down puffy center of heart to allow space for apple filling. Set heart aside to allow to completely cool before filling. Peel apples, and cut in quarters. Remove core area; then slice apples lengthwise very thin. In a large skillet, bring the apples, sugar, water, and lemon slice to a boil. Cover and reduce heat to simmer for 10 minutes. Stir occasionally, and do not allow apples to become brown. Cool apple filling; then place cooled apples inside the pastry heart. Outline edges of pastry heart with the sliced strawberries. All strawberries will not be used; serve them on the side, if desired. Refrigerate any unserved tart.

Magic Blueberry & Pineapple Cobbler

This cobbler is made in layers with no mixing required.

1 (20-oz.) can crushed pineapple in own juice, undrained
3 cups fresh or frozen blueberries

3/4 cup granulated sugar
1 package Duncan Hines yellow cake mix
1/2 cup margarine, melted
1 cup pecans, chopped

Preheat oven to 350 degrees. Prepare a 9- x 13-inch baking dish with spray-oil. Make in layers beginning with undrained pineapple spread on bottom of dish; then blueberries, sugar, dry cake mix, drizzled melted margarine, and pecans. Bake in the preheated oven for 45 to 55 minutes or until lightly browned and bubbly.

Banana Split Ice Cream Topping

1 (20-oz.) can crushed pineapple in juice	3/4 cup pecans, chopped
2 tablespoons granulated sugar	Chopped walnuts (optional)
1 small jar maraschino cherries, sliced and drained	Freshly sliced bananas (optional)

In a medium saucepan, combine the pineapple with the juice and the sugar. Bring to high heat; then reduce heat to simmer for about 30 minutes. Cook until all of the juice has evaporated. Add drained cherries, cut in half, nuts, and banana slices, if desired; gently mix. Serve over ice cream; refrigerate to store. Will freeze.

Ellen Hagood Ellis has made this perfect ice cream topping for many years. You could continue the decadence by splitting a banana, filling the center with 3 scoops of ice cream, drizzling hot fudge or chocolate syrup over the top, and spooning on the Banana Split Topping! Wooooooow, sounds great!

Fabulous Spanish Flan

1-1/2 cups granulated sugar, divided	4 eggs
1 quart milk	1/4 teaspoon salt
	1 teaspoon vanilla

Preheat oven to 300 degrees. In an iron skillet, over medium heat, cook one cup of the sugar, stirring constantly, until melted and light brown. Slowly pour the melted sugar in the bottom of an 8-or 9-inch metal baking pan. Tilt the pan to coat the bottom and sides with the melted sugar; set aside. In a medium saucepan, heat the milk to hot, but not boiling. In a large bowl, beat eggs remaining 1/2 cup of sugar, salt, and vanilla. When milk is hot and the temperature is just below boiling, slowly and vigorously beat the hot milk into the egg mixture. Pour the mixture in the metal pan, and place the pan in a larger metal pan filled with enough water to partially cover sides of the flan pan. Place both pans in the preheated oven, and bake for 50 to 60 minutes. Test with a knife blade; it will come out clean when flan is set. Cool for 30 minutes; then turn flan out of pan on a flat platter with a lip. Refrigerate to chill before serving. Keep refrigerated.

Joe and I both love this recipe. The flan is made old-world style with real milk. It's quite a treat.

Erin's Very Favorite Pralines

Use a candy thermometer. They are inexpensive, and will make your life easier! All ingredients should be handy and measured before beginning candy. Place the aluminum foil-covered pans adjacent to the stove top. When dropping the cooked candy, work quickly to keep candy hot while dropping. If candy cools before dropping, it begins to loose the shiny, glass-like appearance. The candy will still be good, but not quite as pretty. If candy becomes too hard to remove from the saucepan, heat again very briefly to "get it moving."

1 cup granulated sugar	3 tablespoons butter or
1 cup light brown sugar, packed	margarine
1/2 cup Half and Half	2 cups pecans (may use halves,
1/4 teaspoon salt	broken pieces, or chopped)

Cover 2 cookie sheets with aluminum foil, and prepare the foil with spray-oil. In a heavy 2-or 3-quart saucepan, combine both sugars, Half and Half, and salt. Place candy thermometer in the mixture; then heat, and stir constantly to a temperature of 228 degrees. Stir in the butter and pecans. Continue cooking, stirring constantly, to a temperature of 236 degrees. Remove from heat, and beat to cool until candy just begins to thicken. Quickly drop candy by tablespoonfuls on the aluminum foil. Work as quickly as possible; if candy becomes too thick, heat briefly to soften.

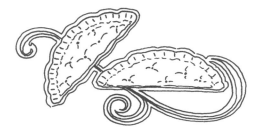

Cliff's Strawberry Ice Cake

Make one day in advance.

1/2 gallon strawberry ice cream
1 (10-oz.) box frozen sliced
   strawberries with juice, thawed

1 (20-oz.) can crushed pineapple,
   drained
2 cups whipped topping
1 large angel food cake
1 cup pecans, chopped

Allow ice cream to come to room temperature. Mix ice cream, strawberries with juice, drained pineapple, and whipped topping. Remove brown crust from the cake, and break cake into small pieces. Stir angel food cake and pecans into ice cream mixture. Pour in a Bundt or tube pan. Freeze overnight. Several hours before serving time, dip the bottom of the pan in hot water, just until sides begin to soften; then invert on a cold silver tray. Return silver tray to freezer to allow any melted ice cream to harden; then clean up any ice cream melt. Cover ice cake, if not being served within the hour. At serving time, allow the ice cake to thaw for 10 minutes before slicing.

Chocolate Nut Clusters

1 lb. mixed nuts, unsalted or
   lightly salted

1 lb. chocolate bark candy

Preheat oven to 325 degrees. Spread nuts on a large baking pan, and roast about 10 minutes or until the nut aroma is released. Melt chocolate bark candy in the top half of a double boiler. Bring water to boiling to begin chocolate melting; then lower heat to keep water hot; do not boil. Stir warm roasted nuts in the melted chocolate coating. Drop by tablespoonfuls on waxed paper, and allow to stand at room temperature until set, about 30 minutes. Makes about 45 to 48 clusters.

Lemon French Puffies

1 package frozen puff pastry shells, thawed	2 egg yolks, beaten
1 cup granulated sugar	1 tablespoon margarine
2/3 cup plain flour	Juice of 1 lemon
1/4 teaspoon salt	Sweetened whipped cream
2 cups boiling water	(optional)

Bake the puff pastry shells exactly according to package directions. Remove tops and the soft pastry underneath, as instructed. Allow shells to completely cool. While shells are cooling, make the lemon filling. In a medium saucepan, mix sugar, flour, and salt; add boiling water, and stir until dissolved. Stirring constantly, cook sugar mixture over medium heat until thickened. Add beaten egg yolks VERY SLOWLY to the hot mixture; then cook on low for about 1 minute. Add margarine and lemon juice; stir until margarine is melted and juice is blended. Cool lemon filling COMPLETELY before spooning into the cooled puff shells. Replace puff pastry tops, and finish with a dollop of whipped cream, if desired. Serves 6.

French Puffies

A just-for-fun recipe from 1689	**Belvior Castle, Leicestershire, Great Britain**

Take a pound of double refin'd sugar, fine sifted. Steep a pennyworth of Gum Dragon in orange flower water one night. Then next day strain it through lawn. Bruise very fine a grain of musk or amber grease, mix it with the sugar, as will make it into a paste, in which strew some little red seeds or comfitts to colour it. The rest make up white. It must be rolled till it be about the bigness of a jumball. Then cast it to what Puffies you please. Lay them very thin upon papers that they may have room to blow up and not touch. Lay then on wairs in a cool oven.

Mary's Fabulous Chocolate Pecan Butter Toffee

A candy thermometer is needed.

1-1/4 cups butter or margarine
  (do not use light)
2-1/2 cups granulated sugar

1 teaspoon salt
1/2 cup water
4 oz. pecans, chopped
4 oz. chocolate bark candy

Line a large baking pan with aluminum foil; then prepare with spray-oil, and set aside. Place a candy thermometer in a heavy saucepan. Add the margarine, sugar, salt, and water; heat and stir until boiling. Add pecans, and continue stirring until candy thermometer reaches 290 degrees. Pour the hot candy on the sprayed aluminum foil, tilt to cover pan evenly. Allow to cool. In a double boiler over boiling water, melt the chocolate bark candy, and make a layer of the hot chocolate over the cooled toffee. Spread the hot chocolate with a rubber spatula over the entire top of candy. Allow candy to completely set and cool before breaking into jagged pieces. Store in an airtight container.

Unfortunately for my waistline, my sister by marriage, Mary Harris Keck, makes this "To Die For" candy. It's truly beyond compare, as her husband James will agree. Not only is she a super cook, wife, and mother, but Mary has been awarded "Teacher of the Year" status from the school where she teaches. The toffee makes a beautiful and delicious gift for any occasion. A labor of love!

Gresham's
Crusty Baked Apple
Goodies

2 Granny Smith apples, unpeeled and washed	1 cup orange juice
1 package 8 refrigerator crescent rolls	1 cup granulated sugar
1/2 cup margarine	Sweetened whipped cream or whipped topping, if desired

Preheat oven to 350 degrees. Prepare a shallow 2-quart baking dish with spray-oil. Cut unpeeled apples in quarters, and scoop out the core area. Open crescent rolls, and separate into 8 pieces of dough. Using the palm of hand, slightly flatten each piece. Form the dough around each apple quarter. Place the wrapped apples in the baking dish. In a medium saucepan, combine all remaining ingredients, and bring to a boil. Pour the hot sauce over the wrapped apples, and bake in the preheated oven for 30 to 40 minutes until golden brown and bubbling. Baste the crust of the apples several times while baking. Top with whipped cream or whipped topping when serving, if desired. Serves 8.

Chocolate & Fruit Sweet Puff Twists

1 sheet of a (17-1/4-oz.) package of frozen puff pastry	2 oz. semisweet chocolate chips
2 tablespoons red plum or strawberry jam	1 egg, beaten
	1 tablespoon water

Thaw pastry sheet. Preheat oven to 400 degrees. Prepare cookie sheets with spray-oil. Place thawed, unfolded pastry sheet on a lightly floured board, and roll out with a rolling pin in a 10- x 14-inch rectangle. Spread a thin layer of the jam over the entire surface of the pastry. Cut the pastry in half lengthwise, and set aside. Place the chocolate chips in a food processor with a steel blade, or in a blender. Turn the machine on and off several times to mince the chocolate chips. Sprinkle the minced chips on one of the half-sheets of pastry. Place the half-sheet with jam only on top of the half sheet with the chocolate. Gently roll with the rolling pin, and press together. Set aside the pastry for 10 minutes to allow to slightly dry. In a small bowl, beat the egg with the water. After the drying time, cut the pastry crosswise into 1/2-inch strips. Using fingers, press together the top of each strip, and the bottom of each strip. Then, twist to resemble a gently curled ribbon. Place the pastry twists at least 2-inches apart on the cookie sheets. Brush the pastry with the egg mixture. Bake in the preheated oven for 10 minutes or until puffed and golden. Twists can be served hot or room temperature. After cooling completely, store in an airtight container to keep crisp. Makes about 28 twists.

Parfait Au Kirsch

Any liqueur may be used. This recipe uses uncooked eggs. Make it if there are no objections to this feature.

2 eggs, separated and room temperature
2 teaspoons granulated sugar
4 tablespoons Kirsch liqueur
1/2 pint whipping cream

In an electric mixer, beat the egg yolks and sugar until a light lemony color. By hand, stir in the liqueur. In another cold mixing bowl, whip the cream until stiff. In a third, room-temperature bowl, beat the egg whites until very stiff. By hand, gently fold the egg yolk mixture and whipped cream mixture into the egg whites, keeping the mixture light and frothy. Fill parfait glasses, and freeze for at least 4 hours. Serve frozen. Makes 4 parfaits. If keeping parfaits frozen for a longer period of time cover with plastic wrap, and secure with rubber bands.

Pecan Almond Roca

Use a candy thermometer.
1 lb. butter (no substitutes)
2 cups granulated sugar
3 tablespoons water
2 cups blanched almond slivers

2 to 3 (12-oz.) packages semi-sweet chocolate chips (no substitutes)
1 lb. pecans, finely ground, or pecan meal

Using a heavy saucepan, bring butter, sugar, and water to register 250 degrees on the candy thermometer. The color is yellow to begin; then turns beige. Stir in almonds and bring temperature to 275 to 300 degrees. Test in a glass of cold water until a firm ball forms. Pour candy in an ungreased 9- x 13-inch or slightly larger baking pan. Allow candy to fill entire pan surface. Almonds will need to be spread to make candy even since it will be broken later. Allow candy to dry overnight in a protected place. The next day, break the candy into pieces. In a double boiler over boiling water, melt 1/2 package of chocolate chips. Add additional chocolate chips, as needed. Dip broken candy pieces into melted chocolate, then into ground pecans. Place on waxed paper to set. Keep candy in a tight container.

Melody's Alaskan Chocolate Bombe-Shell

Make one day in advance. Select any three ice cream and/or sherbet flavors that appeal. Any and all of the selections below may be changed. All of the ice cream or sherbet may not be needed to make the recipe. Refreeze unused portions.

1/2 gallon vanilla ice cream 1 package devil's food cookies, approximately 16 cookies	1/2 gallon Rocky Road ice cream 1 quart rainbow sherbet 1 (6-oz.) bottle Magic Shell

Freeze a 3-quart or 12-cup round or square glass, ceramic, or metal bowl (do not use plastic) for 30 minutes. While bowl is chilling, open a carton of vanilla ice cream, and allow to soften enough to cut in 1-inch slices. Form the slices in the bottom and up the sides of the chilled bowl to make a vanilla ice cream shell. Immediately freeze the shell for 30 minutes; then place all of the cookies in a layer on the bottom, as best you can. Freeze for 1 hour. After 1 hour, make a layer of softened Rocky Road ice cream leaving a well in the center to be filled later. Freeze for 1 hour. After 1 hour, fill the well with the rainbow sherbet. Cover container with waxed paper, then with aluminum foil; freeze overnight. Several hours before serving time, dip the bottom of the bowl in hot water for 30 seconds; then invert on a cold silver tray. Return tray to freezer to allow any melted ice cream to harden; then clean up any ice cream melt. Cover bombe if not to be served within the hour. At serving time, use the entire bottle of Magic Shell to cover the ice cream bombe. Cut in wedges to serve. Cover and freeze any unserved portion. Serves 15.

My newest daughter, Melody Noles Westbrook, developed this "cool" dessert. And she says she can't cook! It is spectacular in appearance and flavor, unless your freezer is not cooling properly. Then, the Bombe looks like a Salvador Dali painting! And you look like The Scream by Edvard Munch! Hopefully your freezer is in top running order.

chris'
chocolate critters

3 cups small pecan halves
1 (14-oz.) package caramels,
   unwrapped
	4 (2-oz.) squares chocolate
	   bark candy

Preheat oven to 325 degrees. Prepare cookie sheets by spraying heavily with spray-oil; also spray a metal spatula and wire rack to use later. On the cookie sheets, arrange 5 pecan halves for each individual candy to resemble a creeping Critter. Use one pecan as the head, and four pecans at angles to resemble legs. Place a caramel that has had wrapping removed in the center of each pecan cluster. Bake in the preheated oven for 8 to 10 minutes or until caramels are melted. Place a sheet of waxed paper on the counter under the greased wire rack. When caramels are melted, remove pan from oven; and lift the Critters with the greased spatula onto the greased wire rack to cool. In a double boiler over boiling water, melt the chocolate bark candy; stir occasionally. Keep the chocolate hot over hot water while spooning the melted chocolate over the melted caramel. Allow a small area on the pecans of each candy to remain uncovered with chocolate to make the Critter legs visible. Makes 20 to 40 candies, depending on pecan size.

Death by Chocolate

8 Heath or Skorr candy bars
1 box (19 or 21-oz.) brownie
    mix, baked by package
    directions
1 (3.5-oz) package instant
    chocolate mousse, or
    instant chocolate pudding
    mix, prepared by package
    directions

1 (12-oz.) container whipped
    topping
Stemmed red maraschino
    cherries for decoration

With a rolling pin, crumble candy bars while still in packages. Set a few crumbled pieces aside for garnish. In a large glass or trifle bowl, break half of the brownies in pieces, and place in bottom of bowl. Cover brownies with half of the prepared mousse or pudding, half of the crushed candy, and half of the whipped topping; repeat. Decorate with a few candy pieces, and stemmed red cherries. Serves 20 to 24.

Parisian Puffs

1 sheet of (17-1/4-oz) package
    frozen puff pastry sheets
6 fresh strawberries, washed
6 tablespoons semi-sweet
    chocolate chips

6 tablespoons chopped pecans
Powdered sugar

Preheat oven to 425 degrees, thaw pastry sheet, and unfold. Place pastry on a lightly floured board, and roll with a rolling pin to a 12-inch square. Cut in 6 equal pastries. Roll each pastry with a rolling pin, as thin as pastry can stretch. Slice 1 strawberry into 4 slices, and place in center of 1 pastry. Top with 1 tablespoon chocolate chips, then 1 tablespoon chopped pecans. Bring pastry corners together, just above pecans, and twist "neck area" to turn and seal. Press the loose, pointed corners to fan out slightly. Repeat with all pastries. Place pastries on an ungreased baking sheet. Bake in preheated oven for 10 to 15 minutes or until golden brown. Allow to stand 10 minutes; sprinkle with powdered sugar. *sugar & spice page 241*

Index

Acknowledgements

My Very Special Thanks

To the Ellis Family for giving me the opportunity to write this cookbook for your company. I have worked closest with Ellen Ellis Burkett and have found that whatever I needed was provided quickly and enthusiastically. Even to recipe testing on long, hot days in Priester's huge kitchens. Somehow, there never seemed to be a problem with Thomas, Ellen, or any of the Ellis Family at sampling time! It has truly been a most pleasant endeavor to work with all of the Ellis Family.

To my husband, Joe, and our three children Genia, Almand, and Jay, plus our newly acquired children, Gary and Melody -- I love you all. Your love and loyalty to me are always supremely appreciated and unfailing. I DO lead you all on a "merry-chase" occasionally!

To my mother, Eugenia Judkins Sparks (Gene), more than a mere thank you is due here. From recipe testing, market shopping from a very long ingredients list, errand running, and days of proof reading, I couldn't have done any of this without you.

To my husband's mother, Ann Corcoran Harris -- your support and assistance to me through our many years are especially appreciated.

To the Honorable Craig Cornwell, a Green family member-- your history, written several years ago, about the Priester's Pecan Company was of invaluable assistance in my research on the company. I would have liked to have been able to include a few more pages of your work!

To all of the cookbook contributors -- you realize this great collection of recipes would not have come into being without your participation in making our culinary lives more interesting:

John Andrews, Joan Backes, Carolyn Bailey, Christopher Baye, Hamilton Beggs, Lola Beggs, Ellen Burkett, Willie Butts, Debbie Carden, Greg Carden, Helen Carden, Nancy Carlan, Alice Cheers, Bob Cheers, Gary Clements, Genia Clements, Marsha Cook, Patsy Davis, Ann DeYonker, Nancy Leigh Douglas, May Ellis, Melissa Ellis, Ned Ellis, Thomas Ellis, Juliette English, Beth Fulghom,

Cynthia Godbold, David Godbold, Edward Godbold, Betty Green, May Green, Marshall Green, John Gresham, Julia Mae Gresham, Leonard Gresham, Marjo Gresham, Elizabeth Hall, Elizabeth Harrell, Ann Harris, Juliet Henderson, Jack Hinde, Mitzie Hinde, Ginny Hudson, Susan Jones, Von Jones, Jo Jordan, Madie Keck, Mary Keck, Amy Killingsworth, Dorothy Kuerner, Betty Law, Irene Logan, Marshall Logan, Winnie Long, Sue Ellen Martin, Jo Mikell, Mike Mikell, Karen Newton, Jay Payne, Liza Peterson, Bruce Pfeiffer, Cecelia Pfeiffer, Debby Pfeiffer, Woody Pfeiffer, Eddie Pope, Sue Pope, Betty Powers, Diane Presley, Mike Presley, Cemira Price, Jane Quint, Sara Reddoch, David Rennekamp, Karen Rennekamp, Alice Roberts, Nancy Robinson, Ina Rosser, Kathleen Ryals, Katrina Scofield, Becky Sigler, Mandy Smith, Gene Sparks, Linda Sparks, Scotty Sparks, Tommy Sparks, Wayne Thompson, Almand Westbrook, Jay Westbrook, Joe Westbrook, Melody Westbrook, Lucile Williams, Sherie Wilson, Toneia Young.

Recipe Test Cooks

Lorraine Brutton, Ellen Burkett, Laura Burkett, Tina Campbell, Gary Clements, Genia Clements, Cis Godbold, Virginia Martin, Georgia McKeithen, Queen Pierce, Cemira Price, Annette Riley, Eve Skipper, Lucille Smith, Gene Sparks, Almand Westbrook, Jay Westbrook, Joe Westbrook, Melody Westbrook, Lucile Williams, Sherie Wilson.

Taste Testers at Priester's Pecan Company

Carolyn Adams, Annie Lee Bailey, Jessie Barganier, Elisa Bruner, Lorraine Brutton, Dianne Burkett, Ellen Burkett, Laura Burkett, Ron Burkett, Willie Butts, Rose Cassady, Cathy Dailey, May Ellis, Melissa Ellis, Ned Ellis, Thomas Ellis, Juliette English, Annie Jewel Garrett, Jerry Mae Garrett, Julie Gafford, Chelle Hale, Gwendolyn Hare, Kim Harrell, Christine Hayes, Gloria Hickman, Nancy Hinson, Elizabeth James, Kal James, Lenell Jones, Cherry Jordan, Jo Jordan, Bettye McGough, Arthur McMeans, Bobby McMeans, Cemira Price, Edna Reeves, Barbara Scott, Cindy Sellers, Gerald Sexton, Donna Stokes, Denise Taylor, Dorothy Taylor, Thelma Taylor, Yvonne Taylor, Johnnie Teart, Emma Tolliver, Victoria Tolliver, Janice Whittington, Toneia Young, and all Ellis Family grandchildren

About the Page Illustrator

Gary W. Clements is quite an accomplished illustrator and designer. He was the art director for a large national publishing house for over 20 years. He now owns Quick Draw Studios, a graphic art company. Gary has given the unique Victorian visual touch to the cookbook pages.

Mail-Order Catalog Form
PRIESTER'S
P. O. Drawer 381, Fort Deposit, Alabama 36032

To receive your **FREE COPY of**

PRIESTER'S MAIL-ORDER CATALOG

Featuring:

Our Complete Line of Fine Pecans in all Sizes and Holiday Gifts of:

- **Gourmet Candies**
- **Sugar-Free Candies**
- **Green Tomato Pickles**
- **Pecan Pies**
- **Roasted Nut Varieties**
- **Gift Baskets**
- **Cakes & Fruit Cakes**
- **Jams & Jellies**
- **Gift Tins**

Print Name_____

Address _____

City _____State_____Zip _____

TOLL FREE ORDER: 1-800-277-3226   **FAX: (334) 227-4294**

To receive your **FREE COPY of**

PRIESTER'S MAIL-ORDER CATALOG

Featuring:

Our Complete Line of Fine Pecans in all Sizes and Holiday Gifts of:

- **Gourmet Candies**
- **Sugar-Free Candies**
- **Green Tomato Pickles**
- **Pecan Pies**
- **Roasted Nut Varieties**
- **Gift Baskets**
- **Cakes & Fruit Cakes**
- **Jams & Jellies**
- **Gift Tins**

Print Name_____

Address _____

City _____State_____Zip _____

TOLL FREE ORDER: 1-800-277-3226   **FAX: (334) 227-4294**

To receive your **FREE COPY of**

PRIESTER'S MAIL-ORDER CATALOG

Featuring:

Our Complete Line of Fine Pecans in all Sizes and Holiday Gifts of:

- **Gourmet Candies**
- **Sugar-Free Candies**
- **Green Tomato Pickles**
- **Pecan Pies**
- **Roasted Nut Varieties**
- **Gift Baskets**
- **Cakes & Fruit Cakes**
- **Jams & Jellies**
- **Gift Tins**

Print Name_____

Address _____

City _____State_____Zip _____

TOLL FREE ORDER: 1-800-277-3226   **FAX: (334) 227-4294**

Cookbook Order Form
PRIESTER'S P. O. Drawer 381,   Fort Deposit, Alabama 36032

Please send me_____copies of **DINING ON THE VICTORIAN VERANDAH**
(Includes Postage & Handling)   @ $ 17.75 each   _____
(Or 3 for $49.95)   _____

                                                      Total Enclosed   _____

Print Name_____

Address _____

City _____State_____Zip_____

Check or Money Order to: **Priester's** or Charge to:

Visa___ MC___Diner's Club/ Carte Blanche___ Discover_____ American Express_____

Acct # _____Exp. Date_____

Print Name_____

Phone (___)_____ Signature_____

     TOLL FREE ORDER: 1-800-277-3226   FAX: (334) 227-4294

Please send me_____copies of **DINING ON THE VICTORIAN VERANDAH**
(Includes Postage & Handling)   @ $ 17.75 each   _____
(Or 3 for $49.95)   _____

                                                      Total Enclosed   _____

Print Name_____

Address _____

City _____State_____Zip_____

Check or Money Order to: **Priester's** or Charge to:

Visa___ MC___Diner's Club/ Carte Blanche___ Discover_____ American Express_____

Acct # _____Exp. Date_____

Print Name_____

Phone (___)_____ Signature_____

     TOLL FREE ORDER: 1-800-277-3226   FAX: (334) 227-4294

Please send me_____copies of **DINING ON THE VICTORIAN VERANDAH**
(Includes Postage & Handling)   @ $ 17.75 each   _____
(Or 3 for $49.95)   _____

                                                      Total Enclosed   _____

Print Name_____

Address _____

City _____State_____Zip_____

Check or Money Order to: **Priester's** or Charge to:

Visa___ MC___Diner's Club/ Carte Blanche___ Discover_____ American Express_____

Acct # _____Exp. Date_____

Print Name_____

Phone (___)_____ Signature_____

     TOLL FREE ORDER: 1-800-277-3226   FAX: (334) 227-4294